OVER CALIFORNIA

OVER CALIFORNIA

Text by Kevin Starr

Photography by Reg Morrison

Collins Publishers

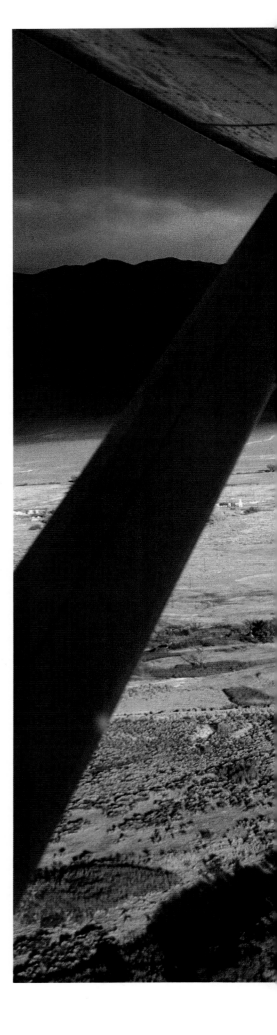

A WINGS OVER AMERICA™ Project

First published in 1990
by Collins Publishers, Inc., San Francisco

Copyright © 1990 Weldon Owen Inc., San Francisco
All photographs (except those credited otherwise)
copyright © 1990 Weldon Owen Inc., available from
WINGS OVER AMERICA™ Aerial Stock Library, 90 Gold
Street, San Francisco, CA 94133. Tel (415) 291-0100,
Fax (415) 291-8841.

Conceived and produced by Weldon Owen Inc.,
90 Gold Street, San Francisco, CA 94133
Tel (415) 291-0100, Fax (415) 291-8841

WINGS OVER AMERICA™ Staff
Publisher: Robert Cave-Rogers
Managing Editor: Jane Fraser
Assignment Editor: Barbara Roether
Copy Editor: Laurie Wertz
Art Direction and Design: John Bull,
   The Book Design Co.
Designer: Tom Morgan, Blue Design
Maps: Mike Gorman
Production Director: Mick Bagnato
Photo Librarian: Ruth Jacobson

OVER™ CALIFORNIA text by Kevin Starr
Principal photography by Reg Morrison
Principal fixed-wing pilot: Michael E. Cummings
Helicopter pilots: Chuck Street (Los Angeles),
   Jim Larsen (San Francisco)

Weldon Owen Inc.
Chairman: Kevin Weldon
President: John Owen
Business Manager: Therese de Veciana-Haddad

Collins Publishers, Inc.
President: Bruce W. Gray
V.P. and Director: Cathy Quealy
V.P., Director of Sales: Carole Bidnick
V.P., Director of Publicity: Patti Richards
Art Director: Jenny Barry
Production Director: Stephanie Sherman

Typesetting by Advanced Typesetting, San Francisco
Printed by Toppan Printing Co., Hong Kong
Production by Mandarin Offset, Hong Kong

Printed in Hong Kong

A Weldon Owen ◆ Production

Library of Congress Cataloging-in-Publication Data:

Starr, Kevin.
   Over California / text by Kevin Starr : photography
by Reg Morrison.
      p. cm.
   "A Wings over America project."
   ISBN 0-00-223703-2
   1. California—Aerial photographs.
2. California—Description and travel—1981–   —Views.
I. Morrison, Reg.   II. Title.
F862.S74   1990
917.94'0022'2—dc20   89–72217   CIP

Above
The fog follows the Santa Monica Mountains in from
the Pacific Ocean.

Right
The Owens Valley stretching below the airplane
wing tip.

Endpapers
Snow geese among the marshes of the Sacramento
National Wildlife Refuge.

Page 1
Point Reyes National Seashore.

Pages 2–3
Located 26 miles off Los Angeles, Santa Catalina is a
21-mile-long island largely preserved as a wilderness area.

Pages 4–5
San Francisco's Golden Gate Bridge at twilight.

Pages 6–7
A film set on Venice Beach reinvents the California
dream.

Page 10
At 2,425 feet, Yosemite Falls is the highest waterfall in
North America.

Page 12
A back road meanders through the Gold Country.

FOREWORD

When I left office as governor of California in 1967, I advised my successor, Ronald Reagan, to spend as much time as possible flying over the great state of California. I advised this not just because of the pleasure involved, but because I had learned such a great deal from my own experiences flying over our state. It's one thing to see California as a set of statistics or as a series of problems coming across the governor's desk; it's quite another thing, however, to experience California from an airplane flying at low altitudes. The statistics suddenly vanish, and there before you in all its glory and variety is the geographical reality of a place called California.

I have just had the pleasure of reexperiencing this vision through the superb photographs of Reg Morrison, the photographer of *Over California*, and through the textual annotations of Kevin Starr, a fine commentator on the California scene.

A great deal has changed since the 1960s, when I was flying "over California." The Los Angeles Basin, where I now live, is more heavily populated, and Sacramento, where I worked as governor from 1959–67, has become a new metropolis. Highways and aqueducts that were in the planning stages when I was in office are now complete; one of these aqueducts, I am happy to say, bears my name. The photos in *Over California* also speak to my personal memories as a Californian. I remember taking my children to the opening of the Golden Gate Bridge in 1937, and hiking as a boy by the Russian River and in the northern woods. I can recall many automobile journeys in the 1930s, 1940s, and 1950s through landscapes which are beautifully presented here.

The most pointed aspect of *Over California*, for me, is the opportunity to view our environment as a dynamic interaction of wilderness, cities, and cultivated landscapes. Regardless of whether we live in the country, suburbs, or cities of this golden state, or whether we are visitors or tourists, it is essential that we respect and preserve the environments presented in *Over California*. Some areas of the state require immediate action if they are to be sustained as wilderness. Other places need to be preserved against future encroachments; still others call for balanced and sensible development.

As each of us plays our part in making these decisions, we must keep the entire state of California in mind. *Over California* reminds me just how vast and impressive my native state really is. It's a wonderful place, and a wonderful book, and I hope you enjoy them both.

Edmund G. "Pat" Brown
Governor of California 1959–67

CONTENTS

OREGON

Crescent City

Klamath
Mountains

Yreka

CASCADE RANGE

Goose Lake

Alturas

MODOC

PLATEAU

Mt. Shasta ▲

Klamath

River

Clair Engle Lake

Eagle Lake

NEVADA

U.S. Route 395

Eureka

Shasta Lake

Redding

Pit R.

I-5

SIERRA NEVADA

Susanville

Honey Lake

COAST

U.S. Route 101

Sacramento

Chico

Lake Oroville

RANGE

Fort Bragg

Feather R.

Yuba R.

Mendocino

River

Clear Lake

THE

Lake Tahoe

Highway 1

Santa Rosa

CENTRAL

I-80

American R.

Placerville

South
Lake Tahoe

Sonoma

Napa

Mokelumne R.

Stanislaus R.

Yosemite

Mono Lake

Berkeley

Stockton

National

San Francisco

Oakland

Tuolomne R.

Park

SIERRA NEVADA

Mammoth
Lakes

Modesto

Merced R.

Palo Alto

San Joaquin

Bishop

PACIFIC OCEAN

San Jose

Merced

Santa Cruz

VALLEY

Death

Monterey Bay

Salinas R.

San Benito R.

Highway 99

Fresno

Mt. Whitney ▲

Monterey

COAST

River

I-5

Valley

Owens Dry Lake

Nation

SAN ANDREAS RIFT ZONE

RANGE

San Luis Obispo

Bakersfield

Cuyama R.

MOJAVE

Santa Ynez R.

Santa Clara R.

Sa

Santa Barbara

Ventura

U.S. 101

Hollywood

Pasadena

I-10

Channel Islands National Park

Santa Monica

R

San Miguel Is.

Los Angeles

Santa Rosa Is.

Santa Cruz Is.

Anaheim

Long Beach

San Nicolas Is.

Santa Catalina Is.

Oceanside

Escond

San Clemente Is.

San Die

14

0   20   40   60
MILES

When Mexico ceded California to the United States in 1848, California included Nevada and much of Utah and Arizona. Pared down to a more reasonable size, California was admitted to the Union in 1850 and is comprised of 158,693 square miles, making it the third-largest state after Alaska and Texas. In 1962 California surpassed New York as the most populous state, a position it still holds.

There are many Californias. The standard division, based on topography and population, is between Northern and Southern California. Because of rapid growth, Central California is in the process of winning equality with the North and the South. *Over California* suggests a new mode of division: one that combines geographic and climatic distinctions with the patterns established by the historical settlement of the state.

The first region of *Over California*, California del Sur and the Central Coast, encompasses that portion of California most heavily settled by Spain and Mexico, the coastal regions of Southern and Central California. The second division, El Dorado, encompasses the first historical phase of American California, the gold rush and the population centers around San Francisco, Sacramento, and the Mother Lode.

The third division, the Natural North, possesses its essential unity in its interlocking structure of mountain, plateau, and forest. The fourth division of *Over California*, the Invented Garden, is coterminous with the Great Central Valley, with some extension into Antelope Valley south of the Tehachapi Mountains. Appropriately enough, this region was also fourth in sequence in terms of irrigation and settlement.

Finally, the fifth division, the Garden Wall, takes into account the two great barriers, the Sierra Nevada and the Mojave-Colorado Desert, which divide California from the Great Basin and make it a region of its own.

The fivefold division of *Over California* seeks to evoke metaphors that are responsive both to the environment and to history. In these photos from the air there unfolds a vast and diverse panorama that represents perhaps the single greatest politically unified environment on the planet and the single most diverse human civilization. To reexperience these natural and man-made images through the eye of the camera is to marvel at how quickly civilization has been achieved in California and yet how powerfully nature maintains its own sublime presence against the human intrusion.

A Crescent City lighthouse guides small boats through the rocky shallows.

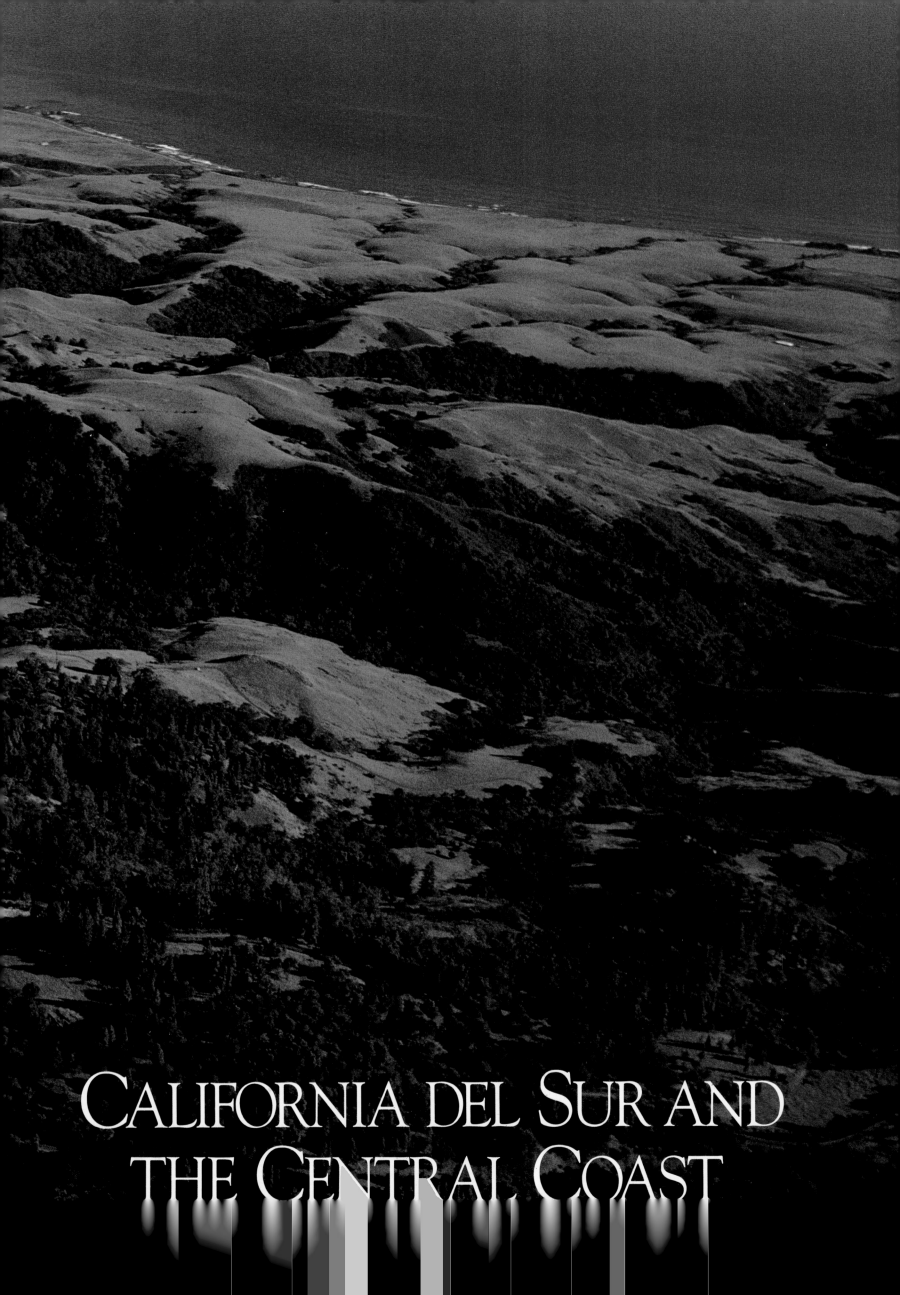

California del Sur and
the Central Coast

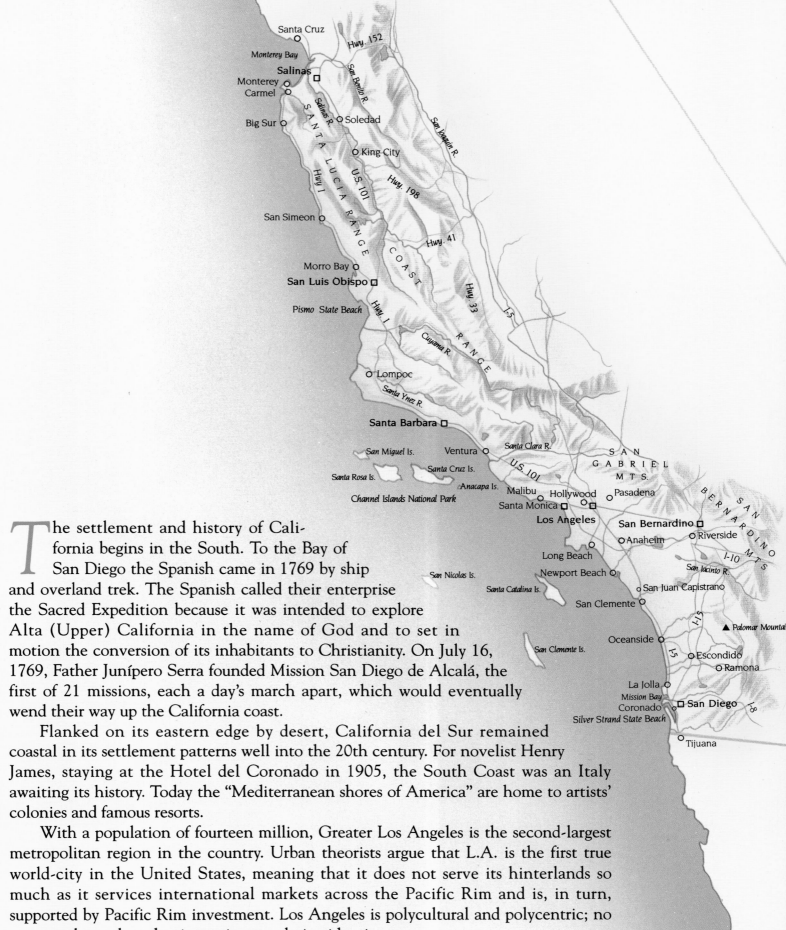

The settlement and history of California begins in the South. To the Bay of San Diego the Spanish came in 1769 by ship and overland trek. The Spanish called their enterprise the Sacred Expedition because it was intended to explore Alta (Upper) California in the name of God and to set in motion the conversion of its inhabitants to Christianity. On July 16, 1769, Father Junípero Serra founded Mission San Diego de Alcalá, the first of 21 missions, each a day's march apart, which would eventually wend their way up the California coast.

Flanked on its eastern edge by desert, California del Sur remained coastal in its settlement patterns well into the 20th century. For novelist Henry James, staying at the Hotel del Coronado in 1905, the South Coast was an Italy awaiting its history. Today the "Mediterranean shores of America" are home to artists' colonies and famous resorts.

With a population of fourteen million, Greater Los Angeles is the second-largest metropolitan region in the country. Urban theorists argue that L.A. is the first true world-city in the United States, meaning that it does not serve its hinterlands so much as it services international markets across the Pacific Rim and is, in turn, supported by Pacific Rim investment. Los Angeles is polycultural and polycentric; no one people or place dominates its cumulative identity.

Farther north lies the Central Coast, divided into three parts. The first part is the region between Santa Barbara and San Luis Obispo, which is classic Spanish country, *la tierra adorada*. The second is the wild Big Sur coastline north of Morro Bay, and the third is the region dominated by Monterey and Salinas.

Previous pages

Julia Morgan designed Hearst Castle at San Simeon for William Randolph Hearst.

The Pismo Beach jetty is a perfect place to watch the surf.

SAN DIEGO

San Diego and the South Coast support a built environment that recapitulates the past and envisions the future of the region. As the twin city of San Diego, Tijuana mirrors the city across the border in Mexican terms, like a family relative who refuses to be forgotten. Is such a border really possible? Can a final line of demarcation be drawn between California del Sur and the first European people who settled it? Tijuana is California del Sur with a Mexican accent—the past that is also the demographic future as the destinies of the two cities become more and more interconnected.

Point Loma Lighthouse commemorates the first European to voyage to *El Norte*. Landing at San Diego in late September 1542, the Portuguese-born captain Juan Rodríguez Cabrillo sailed to present-day Fort Ross in the first reconnaissance of the California coast. Thirty-two years earlier, in 1510, the Spanish romance writer Garcí Ordóñez de Montalvo had surveyed California in imagination only, writing of it as a "Terrestrial Paradise, an island to the right of

Left: Mission San Juan Capistrano preserves the Spanish legacy of California del Sur. *Above:* San Diego Bay separates San Diego from the peninsula resort community of Coronado.

the Indies," peopled by beautiful Amazons ruled by a queen named Calafia. When Spanish explorers sent by Hernando Cortés, conqueror of Mexico, arrived in Baja California in 1533, they believed the peninsula to be an island somewhere to the southwest of the fabled cities of Cibola, and so they named the place "California" in recognition of Montalvo's romance.

Beginning with San Diego, California del Sur functioned as the staging ground for the settlement of Spanish California. Around the mission and pre-

Below: Mission San Diego de Alcalá, established in 1769, was the first Spanish settlement in Alta California.
Right: International commuter traffic increases annually between Tijuana, Mexico, and San Diego, USA.

sidio (army garrison) at San Diego a small adobe town grew up in the early 19th century, and dons and vaqueros began to run their longhorned cattle on the coastal hills, selling their salted hides to Yankee traders.

Despite these trading contacts, San Diego receded in importance to the settlements at Los Angeles, Santa Barbara, Monterey, and San Francisco during the Mexican era, 1822 to 1846. Not until the early part of the 20th century would San Diego reassert itself alongside its counterparts to the north. The vehicle of this self-assertion, the architecturally stunning Panama-California Exposition of 1915, boosted the population of San Diego to more than 100,000, thereby promising the suburbanization that would occur in the region after World War II.

The exposition also left behind a cluster of red-tiled, creamy white buildings at Balboa Park, testimony to the ease with which the residents of California del Sur envisioned themselves as citizens of a sun-oriented culture. Only on Sicily or the North African coast, the Costa Brava of Spain or the Côte d'Azur in the south of France, they argued, could there be enjoyed comparable intensities of mountain, seashore, and sunlight. "Here disease and death may be kept at bay," wrote Doctor P.C. Remondino in the preface to *The Mediterranean Shores of America* (1892), "and life enjoyed to the end of the term of man's natural existence."

California del Sur remains a coastal resort culture. Erected in 1888 as a 399-room seaside resort on little more than a spit running between San Diego Bay and the Pacific, the Hotel del Coronado hosted visitors from the East—Henry James, President Eliot of Harvard, the children's writer L. Frank Baum, creator of the Oz books—for leisurely stays of a week to a month. The Coronado still stands, a rambling Queen Anne wedding cake, to recall the emergence of California del Sur as a national resort.

The United States Navy steamed into San Diego harbor in force during World War I and never left. San Diego became California's preeminent Navy town, and on weekends the Hotel del

Coronado overflowed with naval officers in dress whites and their ladies in pastel.

The ocean orientation of California del Sur runs through a dozen images. From his summer White House at San Clemente, which later became his refuge when everything collapsed, Richard Nixon could see the surfers, the great grey Navy ships pass-ing south to San Diego or north to Long Beach, and the sailing yachts skimming the sea like white gulls. Sunshine, sky, and flowers, a Spanish villa overlook-ing an azure sea—and within the walls a winter-frozen landscape of bitterness and regret. As beautiful as it is, even California del Sur cannot banish the tragic from human experience.

On yet another sunny day, visitors to the Sea World theme park on Mission Bay stroll across a pavement map of the United States. In the mid-19th century it took six months to make the overland journey to California. The completion of the transcontinental railroad in 1869 reduced the journey to just over a week.

Resort hotels like the del Coronado helped pioneer tennis in the United States. California, which has constructed hundreds of public courts, democratized this originally elitist sport and has produced more than its share of champions. Beginning with May Sutton, who won at Wimbledon in 1907, the roster includes Donald Budge, Maureen Connolly, Pancho Gonzales, Hazel Hotchkiss, Helen Jacobs, Billie Jean King, Jack Kramer, Alice Marble, Bobby Riggs, and Ellsworth Vines.

The drydock facility at San Diego is
part of the intricate Navy and Marine
Corps presence, which includes 140,000
active-duty USN and USMC personnel.
Hundreds of Navy ships are home-
ported in San Diego.

Important naval installations are
located in San Diego, Long Beach, and
Wilmington—San Pedro. In the interval
before statehood (granted in 1850),
naval officers frequently served as
governors and alcaldes in the California
Territory. Since the early 1900s the
Navy has chosen Southern California as
the major site of its operations.

*L*eft: These performing
orcas at Sea World are
members of a resident
animal population in the
San Diego area. At the
Wild Animal Park in
Escondido (*below*), the
San Diego Zoological
Society maintains an
1,800-acre preserve for
3,000 free-roaming Asian
and African animals,
including these giraffes.
Right: Geometric fields
of ranunculus flowers
blossom north of
Oceanside and emphasize
San Diego County's
position as an important
center of horticulture, seed
packaging, and flower
distribution.

Silver Strand State Park, south of Coronado, is one of hundreds of miles of public beaches found between San Diego and Santa Barbara. California has 1,264 miles of coast, but Southern California enjoys the warmer waters and bright sunshine favored for swimming and sunbathing.

At Torrey Pines State Beach, wet-suited surfers skim toward shore, exultant atop surfboards perfected by researchers at Cal Tech. By the 1960s, surfing had become a popular sport, adopted by many young Southern Californians.

Top: The Mount Palomar Observatory, east of Escondido, features a 200-inch "Hale Reflector" telescope, for many years the most powerful in the world.
Above: Many ranches prosper in the coastal hills of the Pomona Valley.
Right: Spanish Revival design prevails in the seashore village of San Clemente. Richard Nixon used his Casa Pacifica as the western White House during his presidency.

Stars and Stripes, the U.S. entry in the 1988 America's Cup, sails off the coast of San Diego. Skipper Dennis Conner led the catamaran to a controversial victory over New Zealand.

A city oriented to its waterfront, San Diego spreads for twenty miles along the coast. Water-related activities of all kinds—yachting, surfing, swimming, and sailing—are woven into the city's vacationlike lifestyle.

GREATER LOS ANGELES

Defined in its grandest terms, the Los Angeles Basin extends from the Tehachapi Mountains and Antelope Valley in the north to the Santa Ana Mountains in the south. Los Angeles County is the original South California, a region that on the East Coast would have surely become a separate state.

Los Angeles began in 1781 as El Pueblo de Nuestra Señora La Reina de Los Angeles de Porciúncula, a *pueblo* or township authorized by the Spanish Crown. By the 1840s the pueblo was surrounded by orchards and vineyards, forecasting the golden age of orange groves that would soon come. Los Angeles lazed contentedly in the sun during the Victorian era. Not until 1876 was connecting rail service established with San Francisco, and not until 1885 did the Atchison, Topeka & Santa Fe connect L.A. directly to the east. The Boom of the Eighties, as it is now called, changed the region forever. From a ranching society, lingeringly Hispanic in flavor,

Left: The palms of Palisades Park, Santa Monica, march above the Pacific Coast Highway. *Above:* A rooftop pool and another beautiful day in Los Angeles.

Above: Hundreds of volleyball enthusiasts gather for a tournament at Malibu. *Right:* The intersection of Hollywood and Vine was a famous crossroads by the late 1930s. When Capitol Records was planning its headquarters for 1750 Vine in the 1950s, singer Nat King Cole and composer Johnny Mercer suggested a building that resembled a stack of 45-RPM records. The result is visible here.

Greater Los Angeles was transformed into a middle-class utopia.

Americans from the Midwest dominated this first phase of metropolitanization, which peaked in the mid-1920s. Very deliberately, they fashioned Los Angeles as an Anglo-American city. For a brief while, through the post–World War II era, their hegemony held. In the 1960s the United States reformed its immigration laws to equalize Asian and European quotas. War in Vietnam and revolution in Iran set new migrations in motion. By the end of the

1980s Los Angeles had become a world colony.

Today L.A. supports the largest urban Korean population outside Korea, the largest number of Persians in the United States, and more Mexicans than any city after Mexico City. LAX has surpassed Kennedy Airport in New York as the destination of the largest number of immigrants to the United States.

Only the region's many mountain ranges have resisted suburbanization. The remaining landscape, incorporating some 168 cities and towns, is an interlocking grid of suburbs, freeways, boulevards and expressways, shopping centers, mini-malls, and assorted civic centers which only the most skilled urban geographer can define.

More than any other factor, the automobile has determined the suburban forms and lifestyle of Southern California. The automobile is freedom, mobility, and personal choice. In the early years of the 20th century, the "Big Red Cars" of Henry Huntington's famed Pacific Electric Railway fanned out in every direction from central depots in downtown Los Angeles. By 1924, however, there were 400,000 vehicles registered in Los Angeles County alone, and between 1923 and 1943 Los Angeles County built some 8,000 miles of freeway.

The automobile decentralized the urban form in Southern California, making possible a new way of life. One might live at one place, work at another, and on Sundays worship in another place entirely. The city center was replicated in a dozen other places, and the urban form was made dramatically horizontal. Highway 1, the Pacific Coast Highway, integrated a series of coastal communities whose names suggest the repetitive, rhythmic roll of the surf itself—Manhattan Beach, Hermosa Beach, Redondo Beach, Long Beach, Huntington Beach, Newport Beach, Laguna Beach. They constitute a glorious riviera, funky and bohemian at Venice, posh at Palos Verdes, glittering at Newport Beach, suburban at San Clemente.

Thanks to motion pictures and airplanes, Greater Los Angeles moved from an agricultural economy to a postindustrial high-tech economy. By 1926 motion pictures had become the fourth-largest industry in the world and the first basic industry in California, second only to agriculture as a source of employment and revenue. By the late 1920s Los Angeles was also the leader in aviation, with more than 25 airframe and airplane engine manufacturers active in the region, accounting for a billion-dollar industry.

With so many films shot on location here, Southern California became the place Americans knew best after their own hometowns. As Hollywood became the collective daydream of America, this capacity for dreams, fantasy, and acting out seeped into other aspects of the culture as well.

If films spoke to dreams, aviation spoke to the future. Pushing against present limits of design and materials became the be-all and end-all of aviation

Below: In 1904 Abbot Kinney transformed 160 acres of tidal flats into Venice, complete with canals, now a bohemian holdout. *Right*: Opened in 1927, Sid Grauman's Chinese Theatre in Hollywood features a world-famous courtyard bearing the imprints of movie stars' signatures, hands, legs, and feet.

designers and technicians. The arrival of the *Graf Zeppelin* from Tokyo in August 1929 encouraged Los Angeles to envision itself as a major destination point for international air travel. Aviation motifs and materials showed up in the avant-garde designs of Los Angeles architects Rudolph Schindler and Richard Neutra, and in the progressive Case Study houses of the 1940s, as ways of envisioning the lifestyle of Southern California in the postwar era.

The sight of Los Angeles from the air at night is among the marvels of the world. The city spreads before one, a Lake Tahoe of light, a molten lava flow of moving fire. For years only the 28-story City Hall stood above the skyline, the rest of the city being restricted by a severe 150-foot height limit.

LAX is a gate of empire, the equivalent of the Roman Revival train stations in Boston, New York, Philadelphia, and Chicago that once marked how America's inland empire was unified by a national railway grid. For Greater Los Angeles, this Roman signature, so necessary for American cities, has become not the train station or the airport but J. Paul Getty's re-creation at Malibu of a Roman villa at Herculaneum, to which the Oxford-educated oilman left the bulk of his fortune and his priceless collection of Greek and Roman antiquities. If Southern California was an Italy awaiting its history, as Henry James proposed, then Getty endowed this new Italy with an exquisite reproduction of the classical Mediterranean past that sits quite naturally under the Southern California sun, as if it had been there for 2,000 years.

Twenty-seven miles offshore, the Casino on Santa Catalina echoes Roman Capri. Completed in 1929, the circular building on Avalon Bay is a Moorish-Spanish Revival pleasure dome totally in keeping with the luxuriant optimism of the last year

of the expansionist 1920s. Here in the 1930s the big band generation danced away starlit evenings to the sounds of Benny Goodman and Kay Kyser. The rest of the nation, listening in, grew even more convinced that Southern California was a wonderland by the sea.

Because of the magic of Hollywood, the Beverly Hills Hotel, built in 1912, became a national place, its Polo Lounge crisscrossed each evening with celebrities, its poolside chairs draped by day with the tanning flesh of the famous, semi-anonymous behind their sunglasses. Most Southern Californians sought to duplicate the luxury of the hotels—their ability to create a place, hence a time, beyond the ordinary. In Southern California the private home, like the villas of ancient Rome, assumes the status of an art form expressing values of outdoor living and privacy. Not even in the ancient world were so many luxuriant villas created.

Disneyland, too, speaks to this capacity for Southern California to create national and international destination points, albeit on a more democratically inclusive level. Disneyland is an idealized externalization of American identity, social structures, and values: the grandest Chautauqua of them all.

Dodger Stadium, the Rose Bowl in Pasadena, the Coliseum at Exposition Park, the Hollywood Bowl—each offers opportunities for citizens of the horizontal city to compact themselves into near-vertical crowds. In such traditional gathering places, Los Angeles manages for a moment to resemble other American cities. There is a tendency, in fact, to define Los Angeles not by its recognizably American features but by its eccentricities. Watts Towers, for example, consists of three constructivist structures built from discarded metal, seashells, china plates, glass mirrors, and other objects collected over 30 years by Simon Rodia, an Italian immigrant who wanted to express his gratitude to America. Somewhere at the intersection point of Dodger Stadium and the Watts Towers, the Getty Museum and Disneyland, the Beverly Hills Hotel and a funky backyard in Venice, the real Los Angeles can perhaps be found.

Left: A western frontier town sits vacant on a back lot at Paramount Studios. In the 1930s, MGM screenwriter F. Scott Fitzgerald found such empty sets compelling metaphors for the creative process—lifeless stages awaiting the mesmeric illusions of art. *Above*: Set against the Hollywood Hills, each white sheetmetal letter of this landmark sign is 50 by 30 feet.

Above: When Liberace ordered a swimming pool, he wanted it in the shape of a piano. That made perfect sense. A region that had long since featured hot dog stands in the shape of dachshund pups, orange juice stands in the shape of oranges, and restaurants shaped like giant brown derbies could easily assimilate a piano-shaped swimming pool. *Right:* Glen Campbell, on the other hand, preferred a guitar motif for his swimming pool in the Santa Monica Mountains.

*I*n 1920 Walter and Cordelia Knott bought a boysenberry farm near Buena Park in Orange County, twenty miles southeast of L.A. Today, Knott's Berry Farm features numerous shows, displays, exhibits, and rides, including these "Tubs of Fun."

*I*n 1906 the Rodeo Land & Water Company began to develop portions of the Rancho de las Aguas as the city of Beverly Hills. The streets were arranged in graceful curves and planted in palm trees, with the lavish Beverly Hills Hotel as a centerpiece.

Above: Catalina is a popular stopover point for tour ships that embark from Long Beach and San Diego. Private yachts and the huge circular casino mark the entrance to the harbor of Avalon. *Right:* Two kayakers ply the blue waters awash with sea kelp off Avila Beach north of Pismo Beach. One hundred and fifty years ago Aleut kayakers from Alaska, working for the Russians, hunted sea otters in these same waters, bringing the species to near extinction.

*B*etween 1923 and 1943 Los Angeles County built 8,000 miles of highway. In 1940 the Arroyo Seco Parkway to Pasadena was completed, the first unobstructed expressway in the region and a prototype for the hundreds of freeways and countless overpasses that have been built since then.

*T*he *Dragnet* television series familiarized millions of viewers with the imposing facade of Los Angeles City Hall. Dedicated in 1929, the building is crowned with a replica of the Mausoleum of Halicarnassus, one of the seven wonders of the ancient world.

*D*isneyland, in Anaheim, features this fourteen-story replica of the Matterhorn. One of the great wonders of the modern world, Disneyland opened in 1955 with 185 acres devoted to Fantasyland, Frontierland, Adventureland, and Tomorrowland.

*A*erial photography allows probing views into people's lives, such as this glimpse into several backyards in the Watts section of Los Angeles. Minority and ethnic neighborhoods such as Watts often retain a sense of communal identity which is increasingly rare in the suburban sprawls far removed from the inner city. Watts faces major challenges in the fight against drugs and crime. As in the case of the 1965 riots, the stakes are high.

*I*talian immigrant Simon Rodia worked 30 years to build three constructivist towers in Watts. Made of cast-off material—broken china, seashells, bedsprings, broken glass—Rodia's work stands as a monument to the dedication and creativity of one human being. Today the towers are protected landmarks, eccentric but inspiring like Rodia himself, a small man who said that he "wanted to do something big big."

The Getty Museum in Malibu is a replica of a Roman villa which was buried in 79 A.D. by the eruption of Mount Vesuvius. Founded in 1973 by oil magnate J. Paul Getty, the museum houses his collection of Greek and Roman sculpture and European art.

Like a flying saucer, Chemosphere House (*right*), designed by John Lautner in 1960 for a steep hillside on Torreyson Drive off Mulholland, alights on its single concrete column of support. Lautner studied with Frank Lloyd Wright, as one might easily surmise. Since the pre–World War II work of Richard Neutra and Rudolph Schindler, residential architecture in Southern California has tended toward design and material innovation. In Los Angeles the architectural environment allows for a great deal of personal and social expression (*above*).

*F*or 40 breathtaking miles, Mulholland
Drive soars along the crest of the Santa
Monica Mountains between the Pacific
Ocean and Cahuenga Pass. The
Santa Monica Mountains divide the
Los Angeles Basin from the San
Fernando Valley.

*F*orest Lawn Memorial Park in Glendale was begun in 1917 when banker Hubert C. Eaton acquired a property that included a small graveyard. Eaton built America's first theme park cemetery—a Southern California utopia for the departed.

*D*uring the 1980s Orange County grew from two to three million in population, which meant thousands and thousands of housing starts such as these. Already the swimming pools are marching up the hillside. Demographers predict a steady increase of population in California del Sur. Some predictions are as high as 40 million statewide by the year 2020.

*H*undreds of boat docks line the shores of Lake Arrowhead in the San Bernardino Mountains. The area's lakes, evergreen forests, and ski lodges make it a haven for nearby residents.

Right: Natural and man-made oil
drilling, storing, and refining sites result
from rich offshore oil fields, as this
refinery off Long Beach demonstrates.
Above: Anacapa Island, by contrast, the
easternmost of the four Channel
Islands off Santa Barbara, is virtually
uninhabited. *Anacapa* is Chumash for
"mirage" or "pleasing illusion," which
in so many ways perfectly describes
California del Sur.

64

A crisp clear New Year's Day and Michigan meets the University of Southern California at the Rose Bowl in Pasadena. Designed by Myron Hunt, one of the finest architects in Southland history, the Rose Bowl opened in 1923 as the official home of the first collegiate football championship bowl game. Since 1946 the Rose Bowl game has pitted the Big Ten Conference champions against the number one team in the Pacific Coast Conference. The Tournament of Roses Parade that precedes the game goes back to a floral festival begun in 1890. Nationally televised, the parade offers snowbound viewers in the East and Midwest tantalizing views of sunny Colorado Boulevard in Pasadena, down which pours an ever more elaborate array of floral floats and marching bands. Pasadena lies at the base of the San Gabriel Mountains, visible here in the background.

*I*n 1962 Walter O'Malley, president of the Dodgers, built Dodger Stadium north of downtown L.A. He paid for the stadium out of his own pocket. Before the Dodgers moved from Brooklyn, there was some talk that the city was too spread out to become a good baseball town. Thirty years of Los Angeles baseball has proven otherwise.

A clear April evening and a full moon hovers over the endless carpet of light that is nighttime Los Angeles. By the 1920s the spectacle of the city, unfolding in flowing streams of horizontal light, had become a national attraction. Today, these lights shine behind talk-show hosts in the late hours, bringing to the world via satellite the unique magic of the Los Angeles night.

THE BIG SUR COAST

Santa Barbara is the capital of the south central coast. In the Spanish and Mexican eras, two of California's most influential missions, Santa Barbara and San Luis Obispo, and its most extensive ranchos flourished in this area.

North of Morro Bay, the Spanish metaphor vanishes into the sea fog. This wild region of great mountains, headlands, and ocean remains largely unsettled, which is part of the drama of Hearst Castle at San Simeon, rising as it does in complex splendor in the midst of such a pristine region.

North of San Simeon, Big Sur begins. For a hundred miles, the Pacific heaves powerfully against the Santa Lucia Mountains, creating sheer cliffs, hidden coves and beaches, and Amalfi-like views from Highway 1. Only a handful of ranchers have ever homesteaded Big Sur. The Carmel poet Robinson Jeffers described the isolated, morose lives they led in their remote cabins off the Big Sur River. In

Left: The Rainbow Bridge on Hwy. 1 soars across surf-pounded Bixby Creek Cove at Big Sur. *Above:* An imposing solitude opens on the southern rim of Los Osos Valley.

A Mediterranean mansion on Cypress
Point captures the drama of the region.

the 1950s Big Sur became "transcendentalized" as a generation of seekers—Jack Kerouac, John Montgomery, Gary Snyder, Lawrence Ferlinghetti—sought *dharma* and *satori* while hiking through the fog-shrouded canyons.

Big Sur ends at Point Sur south of Carmel, but while the mountains cease, the coast remains empty and mysterious almost into Carmel itself. There Spain reasserts itself in the form of Mission San Carlos Borromeo del Río Carmelo, founded in 1771 by Junípero Serra. Started as an art colony in the early 1900s, Carmel runs rapidly into Monterey, the capital of Mexican California.

The cities of the Central California coast encompass a diverse spectrum of urban possibilities. Santa Barbara and San Luis Obispo are ranching-oriented county seats, each with a mission and a university campus. Carmel remains lost in a seaside pine forest, which is exactly the way residents of that super-self-conscious community prefer it. Pebble Beach is California Rich: polo, golf, luxurious inns. The Seventeen-Mile Drive wends its way past many of the most ambitious seaside mansions in the state and a number of its best golf courses.

When John Steinbeck lived there, Monterey was little more than an overgrown fishing village centered on Cannery Row, where sardines were unloaded and packed into tins. A major aquarium, the gift of industrialist David Packard, dominates Cannery Row these days, and hotels have replaced the saloons and boardinghouses. Despite this development, history still pervades Monterey. From here Mexico governed California, and the Constitutional Convention met here in 1849 to prepare California for statehood.

At the other end of Monterey Bay is Santa Cruz, a lumber center before the University of California located a campus there in the 1960s. The boardwalk at Santa Cruz reminds the university crowd that the town was for decades a beach city for the San Francisco peninsula, connected to San Francisco by a direct railroad line, its cars crowded on the weekends and throughout the summer with revelers heading for the Coney Island of the West.

The agricultural cities of Watsonville, Hollister, Castroville, and Salinas, inland from Monterey Bay, are no-nonsense, hard-working towns. Salinas itself is the epicenter of Steinbeck country, lettuce country, Cesar Chavez and United Farm Workers country.

No wonder this region produced California's best-known (and its only Nobel Prize–winning) novelist. John Steinbeck set nearly all his fiction in this one area, for in geography, places, human types, and social classes, from Carmel to Watsonville, Pebble Beach to Salinas, the Central Coast was, and remains, a most intriguing American place.

Año Nuevo State Reserve, north of Santa Cruz, is an island refuge for thousands of young California sea lions. Hunted to near extinction in the 19th century, the sea lions, along with other native marine mammals, have made a remarkable comeback under protection. Closed to the public, Año Nuevo Island is an important site for research into sea lion and seal breeding habits.

The Pebble Beach Golf Club, north of Carmel, includes some of the most scenic fairways in the country. Players on the seventh hole (*foreground*) sometimes lose their drives to gusty seawinds. The famed Seventeen-Mile Drive winds along the edge of Pebble Beach.

The Santa Cruz Beach boardwalk is the last such old-fashioned amusement park in the state. The rollercoaster is famous for its scary plunge toward the sea.

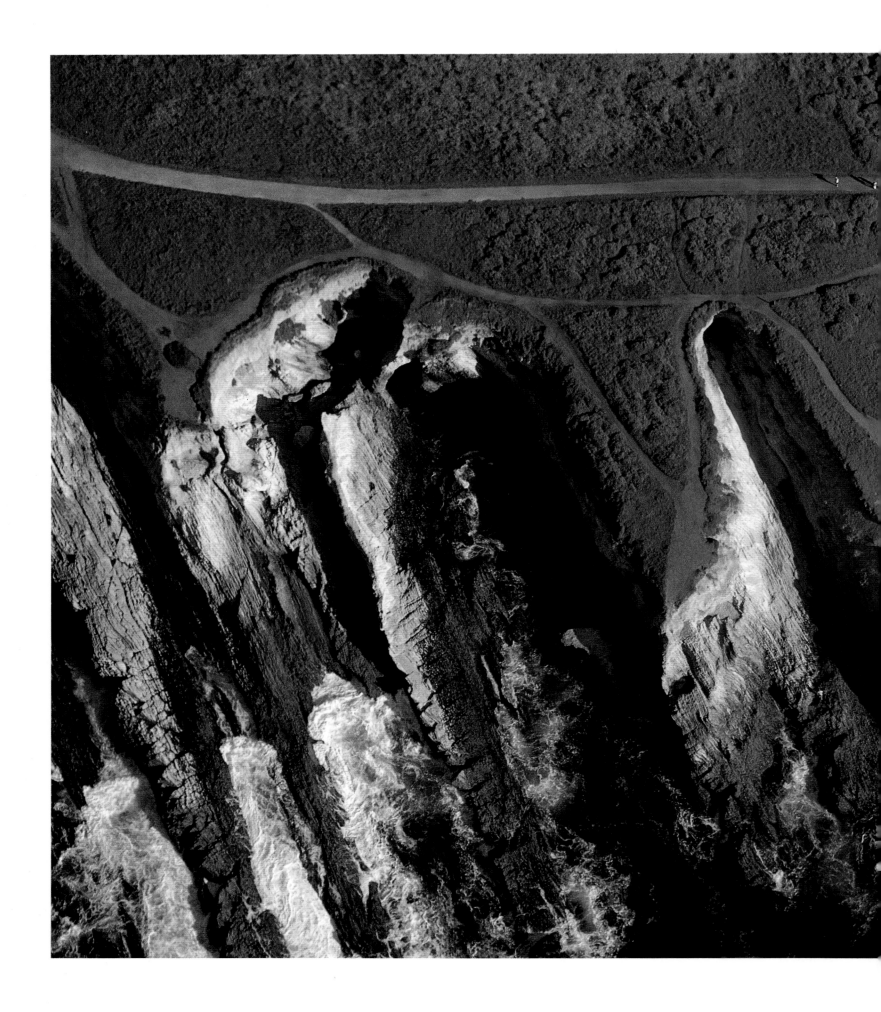

The Central Coast of California becomes more rocky and mountainous as one moves north. Pismo Beach (*above*) in southern San Luis Obispo County is a wide-open beachfront, and dune buggies roam its vast expanse. Farther north, a steep cliffline at Montana de Oro State Park (*left*) crumbles into a rolling Pacific surf. The Southern California metaphor of the beach as a sunny Arcadia changes in the north to an emblem of elemental power and strength.

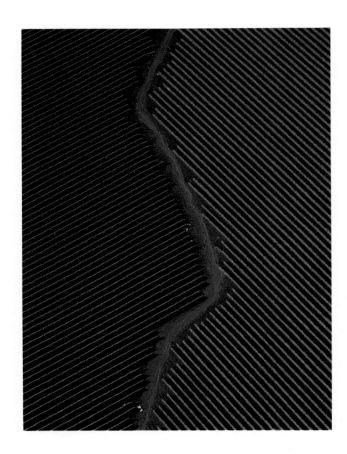

Previous pages

Morro Rock rises 576 feet out of
the ocean to stand guard over Morro
Bay and San Luis Obispo. The rock
is a remnant of an ancient volcano,
now a favored nesting site for
peregrine falcons.

Visitors driving along coastal Hwy. 1
can easily miss the agrarian landscapes
that lie just inland—areas such as the
Salinas Valley, east of Santa Cruz,
where field workers harvest celery in
early November. In some areas on the
Central Coast planted fields of pumpkin
and artichoke extend to the very
shoreline, bringing coastal and farming
life into dramatic juxtaposition.

Left: Part health spa, part garden
retreat, Esalen Institute on the
cliffs of Big Sur has been a center
of experimental philosophy and
psychology since 1962. *Above:* The
coastal city of Santa Barbara emerged
as a popular resort in the 1890s. The
Spanish Revival architecture of the
county courthouse evokes the romance
of Old California.

EL DORADO

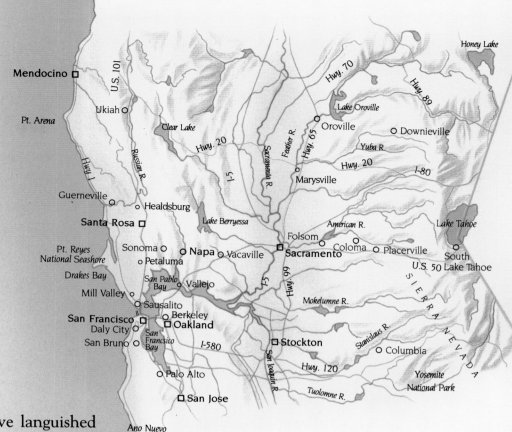

The map shows locations including: Mendocino, Ukiah, Pt. Arena, Clear Lake, Guerneville, Healdsburg, Santa Rosa, Sonoma, Napa, Vacaville, Petaluma, Pt. Reyes National Seashore, Drakes Bay, Mill Valley, Sausalito, San Pablo Bay, Vallejo, San Francisco, Daly City, Berkeley, Oakland, San Bruno, San Francisco Bay, Palo Alto, San Jose, Ano Nuevo State Reserve, Honey Lake, Lake Oroville, Oroville, Downieville, Feather R., Yuba R., Marysville, American R., Lake Berryessa, Folsom, Sacramento, Coloma, Placerville, Lake Tahoe, South Lake Tahoe, Mokelumne R., Stockton, Columbia, Stanislaus R., Yosemite National Park, Tuolomne R., San Joaquin R., Russian R., Sacramento R., Sierra Nevada, U.S. 101, U.S. 50, Hwy. 1, Hwy. 20, Hwy. 65, Hwy. 70, Hwy. 89, Hwy. 99, Hwy. 120, I-5, I-80, I-580

C alifornia might very well have languished for decades as a remote, underpopulated military territory had not carpenter James Wilson Marshall noted on January 24, 1848, a glint in the gravelly tailrace on the South Fork of the American River near the present town of Coloma.

When news of the discovery spread to Sutter's Fort, to San Francisco, and to Washington, D.C., where President Polk announced it officially to Congress in December, the population of California stood at 18,000. More than 60,000 gold-seekers, the forty-niners, arrived in 1849. By 1852, when the gold rush peaked, California had a population of 255,000. More than 100,000 of the recent immigrants, from every corner of the globe, were in the mines seeking the Golden Fleece.

El Dorado is Spanish for "the one covered in gold." It refers to a mythical Indian chief from Colombia whose body was ceremonially gilded in gold leaf. By extension, it came to mean the lands of gold over which El Dorado ruled. The Spanish conquistadors more than half believed that El Dorado existed some place north of Mexico. When gold was discovered in California, mapmakers used the name El Dorado to describe the gold region.

In *Over California*, El Dorado refers to the vast region of Northern California encompassing the San Francisco Bay Area, the counties to the north as far as Mendocino, the delta regions between Stockton and Sacramento, the Sacramento Valley up to Marysville, the counties of the Mother Lode itself, and Lake Tahoe at the crest of the Sierra Nevada.

El Dorado is the geographical and historical heartland of California. Here the two great rivers of the state, the Sacramento and the San Joaquin, drain into San Francisco Bay for discharge into the Pacific. Around the bay has materialized the state's second-largest urban region after metropolitan Los Angeles—encompassing San Francisco, San Mateo, Palo Alto, San Jose, Fremont, Union City, Hayward, Oakland, Berkeley, Richmond, and Vallejo, all so very distinct from one another in texture and sociology, yet unified by one freeway system and the pervading presence of the bay.

El Dorado's oldest settlement, San Jose, founded as a Spanish pueblo in 1777, is its newest boomtown, the third-largest city in the state after Los Angeles and San Diego, in terms of population. Sacramento, premier gold rush city and state capital, is the most recent metropolitan region in California to pass the million mark in population.

R ibbonlike Hwy. 1 skirts the fog-banked crest of the Marin County coast.

Previous pages
T he Golden Gate Bridge floats on fog between Marin and San Francisco.

THE SAN FRANCISCO BAY AREA

The Golden Gate Bridge, a masterpiece of engineering and Art Deco design, links the densely packed city of San Francisco with the still-wild headlands of Marin, forever preserved as the Golden Gate National Recreation Area. The conjunction of cityscape and wilderness offers a perfect paradigm of Northern California.

When Harvard philosopher George Santayana visited California in August 1911 to address the Philosophical Union at Berkeley, he made a telling, and somewhat prophetic, observation concerning Northern Californians and the environment. Northern Californians, Santayana noted, were primarily an urban and suburban people who took nature and the environment, not human settlements, as their primary symbol of identity. This mixed ambience of nature and civilization first noted by Santayana remains an essential component of the Bay Area

Left: Streets of the inner Sunset District proclaim the pervasive grid of San Francisco. *Above:* Architect Irving Morrow made the Golden Gate Bridge a masterpiece of Art Deco design.

style. It expresses itself in a myriad of architectural and lifestyle associations: the shingled homes designed by Bernard Maybeck nestling against the Berkeley hills; the strength of the Sierra Club in the Bay Area, with the archetypal Northern Californian John Muir as its first president; and the extensive parklands and greenbelts throughout the region.

Northern Californians always seem anxious to get away for weekends or vacations to some alternative place—the wild coast north of Marin, the Sierra foothills, the mountain plateaus and lakes of the Far North, or more locally to Mount Tamalpais in Marin or Tilden Park in Berkeley—where nature remains unspoiled, accessible, direct. In the 19th century, Bay Area Californians would go into the mountains for weeks at a time, bringing along elegant tents, camp furniture, oriental rugs, the finest in wine and food.

The naturalist premise of the Northern California lifestyle has originated a number of national trends: the holistic health movement, the physical fitness rage, the anti-smoking crusade, a preference for wines over spirits, nouvelle cuisine, and the more subtle psychological adjustments of the human potential movement.

San Francisco is a festive city, a city so favored by site and climate that enjoyment of life has become its major preoccupation. Even in its busy years as a financial center, San Francisco managed to savor the pleasures of urban life with special intensity. As early as 1849 San Franciscans could dine on oysters and champagne and enjoy a premiere performance of Rossini's *Stabat Mater*. Soon they were congregating in the evenings at some of the finest hotels in the nation, such as the Palace on Market Street, in its time the largest hotel in the western hemisphere. By the turn of the century, San Francisco was calling itself the Paris of the Pacific.

*T*he Transamerica Pyramid on Montgomery Street, designed by William Pereira & Associates, has become a signature building of the San Francisco skyline since its completion in 1972. Rigidly restricted in its expansion, San Francisco contains many ambitious highrises which give the city a compact and dramatic appearance.

The earthquake and fire of April 1906 shook and burned the heart of this *belle époque* metropolis to the ground. Out of its ashes rose another and equally pleasure-loving city. The Palace of Fine Arts in the Marina survives from the Panama-Pacific International Exposition of 1915, which invited the world to come and see a splendid new city that had risen phoenixlike on the shores of San Francisco Bay. Visitors poured in, and three-quarters of a century later they continue to arrive by the millions.

San Franciscans live each day in the company of fog. Like a welcome friend, the fog is often there at dawn, burning off by mid-morning. And in the late afternoon or early evening, when the day's work is done, the fog returns to the city, and is welcomed. Slipping through the narrow streets of Jackson Square or Russian Hill, heading down toward the Tenderloin,

it creates a mood of mystery and expectation, as if suddenly, from out of a doorway, Sam Spade might emerge in trenchcoat and fedora, going after the Maltese Falcon.

While the fog of San Francisco is omnipresent and multishaped, the streets of the city over which it hovers tend to be rigidly geometric. In 1847 Surveyor General Jasper O'Farrell made the first official survey of San Francisco and organized the future city into a geometric grid. His master stroke was having Market Street sweep diagonally across the city, thereby imposing on San Francisco its central boulevard.

Some critics would have preferred that the streets of San Francisco circle around the city's many hills rather than run up and down them in linear lockstep. Others defend O'Farrell's grid, arguing that it provides San Francisco with its own form of rhythmic spatial power. There is literally not a square

San Francisco is a place that loves to be looked at. The city stretches across a long peninsula between the bay and the Pacific Ocean, thrusting its seven hills into the fog-swept sky. The Ferry Building (*left*) at the foot of Market Street survived the earthquake and fire of April 1906.

block in the city that does not contain within its center gridded backlot gardens which themselves form a smaller grid garden. These planted spaces are linked rhythmically with the square plaza parks—Alta Plaza, Lafayette Park, Alamo Square, Washington Square, Union Square, South Park, Dolores Park—that can be found throughout San Francisco. These smaller grid parks, in turn, are linked with such larger entities as Buena Vista Park, Mountain Lake Park, Lincoln Park, Sutro Park, Potrero Hill Park, and St. Mary's Park. This growing synergy of gridded landscapes runs down from Twin Peaks at the center of the city, gathering even greater power in the vast planted spaces—the Marina Green

Right: Having one of the busiest ports in the country keeps the city of Oakland close to the gritty realities of industrial life, which have been virtually banished from San Francisco. *Below:* Bernard Maybeck's Palace of Fine Arts was built for the Panama-Pacific International Exposition of 1915. Today, the Palace houses the Exploratorium.

and Golden Gate Park—which front the bay and the Pacific.

Few cities of comparable size (48 square miles) enjoy such a fruitful array of districts—some of them dramatically different from one another, but only blocks apart. North Beach sustains the ambience of Italy, especially around Washington Square. On Stockton Street in Chinatown one might as well be in the Far East. Japantown, in the Western Addition, was the first successful project by the Redevelopment Agency to be based upon the themes and design motifs of ethnic identity. The city's 100,000-plus Hispanic population has made the Mission District its own special place. There are still pockets of White Russians in the Richmond District and on

Potrero Hill, and the Irish and Soviet Jewish communities are also growing.

Of late the predominant cast of the neighborhoods has become increasingly Asian, since nearly half the resident population is of Asian heritage. The upheavals in Indochina have peopled the Tenderloin District in the heart of the city with an entirely new community of Vietnamese and Cambodians.

Oakland is the hub of the East Bay. If San Francisco is smooth and sophisticated, Oakland is feisty, gutsy, ambitious. Oakland has a world-class port, a great baseball team, an elegant Art Deco downtown, a flourishing Asian community, and the single most

skillful black political establishment in the nation. Today, Oakland is arguably the most successful multiracial city in California, perhaps even in the United States.

Berkeley, Kensington, Albany, and North Oakland take their ambience from the commanding presence of the University of California at Berkeley. Energized by the university, Berkeley has emerged as a truly diverse city, incorporating within its relatively small area such paradoxical constituencies as a large black community, a 30,000-plus student population desperate to find housing, and a central commercial zone supporting some of the most ingenious stores and finest restaurants in the country. Berkeley is perhaps the only city in the United States to have its

Concord, Walnut Creek, Lafayette, Orinda, Moraga, and Martinez are middle-class suburbs which define themselves to a great extent by the very fact that they are not Oakland, Berkeley, or even San Francisco. The same is true of Stockton, the most eastern city that can legitimately be considered part of the Bay Area.

North of San Francisco, across the Golden Gate Bridge, is another legendary Bay Area place, Marin County, which has become identical in the national imagination with the quintessential California lifestyle. Marin begins with Sausalito on the bay, a 19th-century whaling harbor, bohemian-chic in tone. Extending to the northwest are the picturesque and largely mountainous suburban townships of Mill Valley, Ross, Kentfield, San Anselmo, and Fairfax, each of them nestled amidst groves of redwood, oak, and madrone. San Rafael, which began in 1817 as a Franciscan mission, is the most important city in Marin; Novato, on the Marin-Sonoma County border, is Marin's largest bedroom community.

own foreign policy. Beginning with the Free Speech Movement in the mid-1960s, a revolution in attitude and lifestyle occurred here that has had profound ramifications throughout the country.

Far different are the realities of the other suburban cities of the East Bay. Communities such as

Suburban Marin has been satirized as the land of the peacock feather. It is more correctly the land of ten-speed bicycles, Evian water, BMWs and Jeep Cherokees, tennis racquets, barbecues, swimming pools—or any other imagery associated with an exquisitely achieved suburban lifestyle.

In contrast to the woodsy lushness of these communities, West Marin is wild and open, with its mountains rushing to the sea. Stinson Beach, Bolinas, Olema, and Inverness are sea- and windswept villages, almost Nantucket-like in their saline rusticity.

Top left: The two-mile-long Linear Accelerator at Stanford is used for elementary particle research, a branch of physics on the cutting edge of scientific exploration. *Left*: The deep, forestlike calm of the University of California campus at Berkeley belies the institution's tumultuous history. *Above*: The quadrangle to the right of Hoover Tower reflects the architectural uniformity of Stanford's Mediterranean Revival campus in Palo Alto.

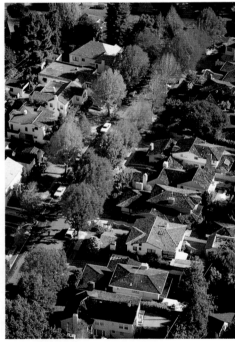

Top: Locally born musician Carlos Santana dominates a mural in the Mission District. *Right:* Moving day brings two vans to a Pacific Heights home on the other side of the city. *Above:* An autumnal street in Alameda conjures up visions of mid-America.

*N*estled against a wooded hillside at the northern end of the Golden Gate Bridge, Sausalito was a haven for whaling ships in the 19th century. In the mid-20th century it became a bohemia of funky houseboats and hillside eyries, its waterfront alive with spars and bars.

Following pages
*O*nce slated to become a housing development, the rugged headlands of Marin on the northern end of the Golden Gate Bridge are preserved as part of the extensive Golden Gate National Recreation Area.

At 8.5 miles, the double-decked San Francisco-Oakland Bay Bridge is the longest steel bridge in the world. Connecting San Francisco with the East Bay cities of Oakland and Berkeley, and the Bay Area's many suburbs, the Bay Bridge carries the bulk of local commuter traffic.

Near Martinez, in the northeastern arm of the San Francisco Bay, a cove offers a quiet harbor for this fleet of mothballed World War II ships.

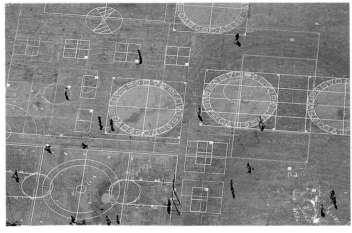

South of San Francisco, in
communities such as Daly City
and San Bruno, tract houses are aligned
above the San Andreas Fault. California
is rife with unusual scenes, yet places
such as this playground suggest
patterns beyond the regional.

The Pacific washes the edge of the
Sunset District on San Francisco's
western shore. The grid of this
residential neighborhood is broken
by the greenery of Golden Gate Park
on the left and Sutro Heights in the
background.

A hang glider circles beneath a World War II gun emplacement at Fort Cronkhite on the Marin headlands north of San Francisco. Sheer launch points, active winds, and soft beach landing sites make these cliffs a favorite place for this popular sport.

*E*ast Brother Light Station on San Pablo Bay testifies to the care with which the Lighthouse Service established itself in the 19th century around San Francisco Bay. One of the major installations of its era, it guided traffic to and from the Carquinez Strait.

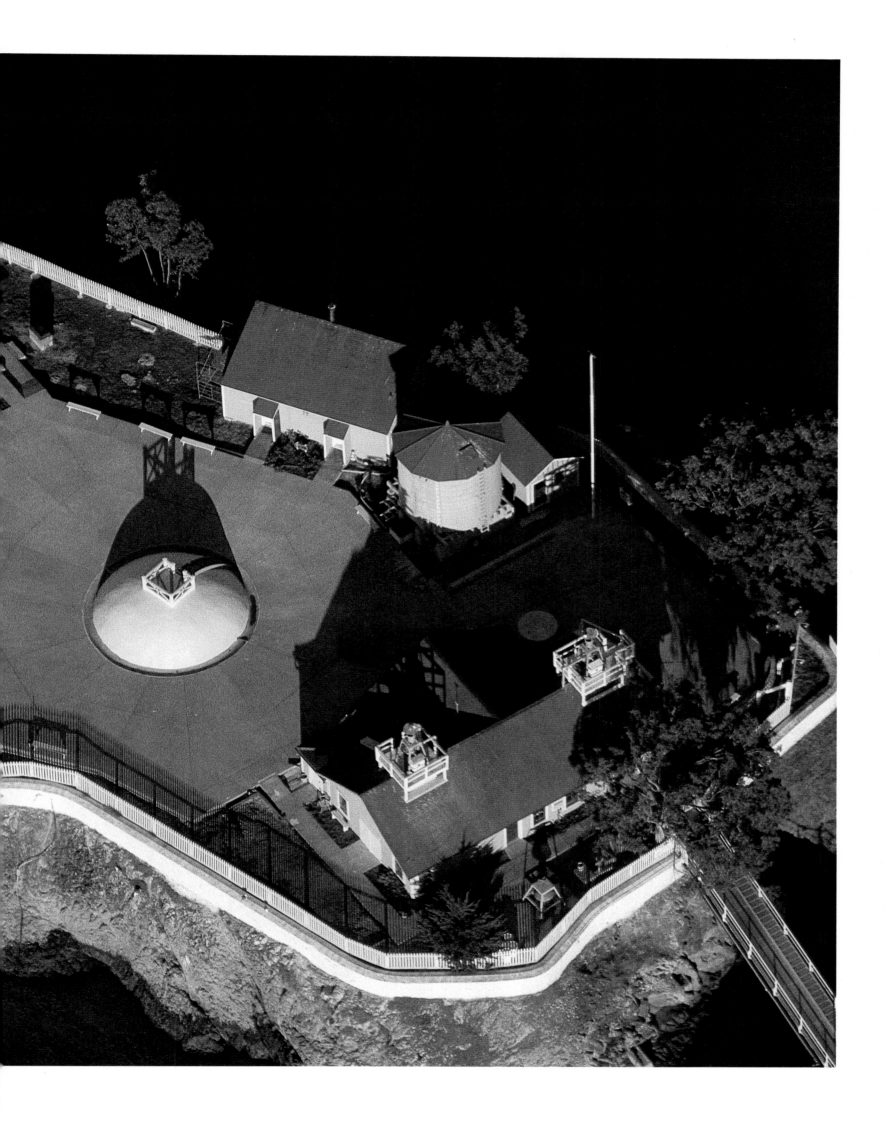

SAM SARGENT PHOTOGRAPHY

EARTHQUAKES

California shares with its Pacific Rim neighbors the ever-present threat of seismic cataclysm. Like Japan, parts of eastern China and Russia, the Philippines, and the coasts of Central and South America, California is part of the vast circle of geologically unsettled lands around the Pacific, a circle that closely parallels the volcanically restless Ring of Fire. Each year 20 to 30 major earthquakes occur somewhere on the planet, 90 percent of them in this zone.

Most earthquakes are caused by the movements of the fifteen tectonic plates (landmasses) that form the earth's surface. Some plates tend to grow at their edges, pushing the neighboring plates away; some slip underneath neighboring plates. In California, the Pacific Plate and the North American Plate skid against each other in one of the greatest geological traffic jams in the world. The result is the San Andreas Fault or Rift Zone, one of the planet's largest known faultlines. The San Andreas can be traced to origins beneath the Gulf of California. It comes ashore in the Imperial Valley east of San Diego, crawls north past San Bernardino, turns left at the Tehachapi Range, and continues north to San Jose. It edges along the western part of San Francisco and angles in a northwesterly direction to Point Mendocino, a total distance of more than 600 miles. On the western side of the fault, the Pacific Plate tends to push northward, creating a line of tension that eventually tears loose and causes the earth to shake from the rebound.

In the great San Francisco earthquake of 1906, which measured 8.3 on the Richter scale, the plate jumped over twenty feet to the north. The results were catastrophic: the city crumbled, burst gas mains ignited, and 700 people lost their lives.

San Francisco fared somewhat better in the 7.1 temblor (over 20 times less severe than in 1906) that shook the Bay Area on October 17, 1989. About 67 deaths were recorded, though thousands were left homeless. The relatively moderate losses were largely due to San Francisco's strict earthquake building codes; earthquakes in the San Fernando Valley in Southern California during the 1970s led to the statewide upgrading of public structures. Tragically, a stretch of freeway that had not been properly reinforced caused most of the deaths in the 1989 quake.

While California certainly earns its reputation as earthquake country, the rest of America should not forget the great quake of New Madrid, Missouri, in 1811, which forever altered the course of the

Right: Like a scar over an ancient wound, the San Andreas Fault is visible on the surface of the Sacramento Valley. *Above:* The earthquake on October 17, 1989, shook loose a section of roadway on the San Francisco–Oakland Bay Bridge.

Mississippi River, or the Charleston quake of 1886, felt throughout the East. In 1985 New York City was the site of a "4-pointer," and seismologists foresee the possibility of more East Coast quakes in the next twenty years. The earthquake of 1989, which was instantly witnessed by television viewers worldwide, serves as a disquieting reminder that despite our carefully constructed cities and borders, all of us live together in the flux of the natural world.

BARBARA ROETHER

THE WINE COUNTRY

Centered on three adjacent counties—Napa, Sonoma, and Mendocino—the wine country of Northern California has made the transition from an unpretentious agricultural region to a super-chic European-style resort area. The wine country has always attracted international attention. Its most famous visitor has been Robert Louis Stevenson, who married a daughter of the region in May 1880 and honeymooned with her on the slopes of Mount St. Helena, later writing of his experiences in the charming idyll *The Silverado Squatters*. The wine-makers of Stevenson's era tended to be Yankee ranchers, with an exotic European or two thrown in, such as the redoubtable Agoston Haraszthy, a Hungarian count who established the Buena Vista

Left: Inglenook winery in Napa County is part of the Vineyard of the West. *Above:* Surrounded by vineyards, Napa remains a quiet town.

Winery in Sonoma in 1856. Commissioned by the state legislature, Haraszthy spent 1861 in Europe, investigating soils and grapes. His report, *Grape Culture, Wines and Wine-Making, with Notes upon Agriculture and Horticulture* (1862), is the founding text, the sacred screed, of California viticulture.

The second generation of Northern California winemakers was comprised of Euro-Californians who expanded the small ranching operations of the first generation. They built stone cellars and châteaux reminiscent of Europe on their properties. Throughout the 1980s a new generation of Euro-Californians, or European investors such as the Rothschilds, have founded new companies or purchased the vineyards and wine cellars of existing operations.

of July parade forms in a square first laid out by Spanish soldiers.

At Monte Rio, sun-lovers soak up the Sonoma sun on the shores of the Russian River adjacent to the famed Bohemian Grove. From here the Russian River has only a few miles to go before it flows into the Pacific at Jenner. North of Jenner is Fort Ross, outpost of the Russian American Fur Company in the early 19th century.

Perched on a fog-shrouded promontory, the town of Mendocino sits like a New England village with the ocean, oddly, on the wrong side of the horizon. Empty, mountainous, heavily forested, Mendocino County is a place preserved from time, the Big Sur of the North.

Fort Bragg on the coast is the capital of one Mendocino: forested, foggy, and mountainous. Ukiah, in the interior, is the capital of the eastern half of Mendocino County. Here the forest relinquishes its dominance to rolling oak-dotted hills, rounded and lion-colored, and the sea fogs give way to the warm sunshine of the Redwood Valley.

The eclectic activities of the wine country on the Fourth of July suggest a midsummer idyll, sunsplashed and serene, extending from inland vineyards to the surf-sprayed sea. A hot air balloon floats lazily over the terraced vineyards of Napa Valley. The Sterling Winery, rising on a hillside like a village on a Greek island, invites picnickers and samplers of vintages. In the city of Sonoma, a Fourth

*E*xtending 40 miles from San Pablo Bay north to the Mayacmas Mountains, the Napa Valley has been shaped by a hundred years of cultivation. Each winery in this verdant garden sustains its own ambience. The Sterling complex (*above*) resembles a whitewashed Greek village.

ROBERT CAMPBELL PHOTOGRAPHY

Above: Fourth of July in Sonoma and the parade files past the Sonoma city square. Founded in 1835 by General Mariano Vallejo, Sonoma has kept at its center a Spanish-style open plaza. About an hour's drive north of San Francisco, Sonoma preserves a small-town atmosphere. *Right:* By contrast, Santa Rosa, the county seat, is en route to full urban status. The Sonoma County Fair, held each summer, is famous for its horseracing, Scottish Games, and carnival rides. For much of Sonoma County, Norman Rockwell's America is as real as ever.

Previous pages
*F*all color decorates the slopes of Mount St. Helena in Napa County. Robert Louis Stevenson wrote of the fog and the mountain in *The Silverado Squatters,* "It was to flee these poisonous fogs that I had left the seaboard and climbed so high among the mountains. And now, behold here came the fog to besiege me in my chosen altitudes...."

ROBERT CAMPBELL PHOTOGRAPHY

*I*n the late 1800s the area's winemakers
were recent émigrés from the wine
regions of France, Italy, and Germany.
After World War II city-dwellers edged
into the business, often on a part-time
basis. By the 1970s many smaller wineries were producing award-winning
vintages and providing their owners
with a gracious lifestyle in the sunny
vineyards of El Dorado.

*F*irst settled in the 1850s, Healdsburg, north of Santa Rosa, has long been a grape-growing center. Within the past two decades, many fine wineries have been established in and around Healdsburg, capitalizing on the nearby Alexander Valley. Service buildings in the area have created a new genre of rural architecture, rustic yet elegant—like the wine country itself.

A horse ranch near Petaluma, in Sonoma County, can trace its origins to General Mariano Vallejo's rancho, established in 1836. Today Petaluma is much more famous for its chickens than its horses.

A farm on the coast near Point Arena stands oblivious to the erosion that slowly claims the homestead of the original settlers.

*A*bove: Winding past Guerneville, Northwood, Monte Rio, and the Bohemian Grove, the Russian River heads toward its rendezvous with the Pacific at Jenner. *Right:* A solitary traveler on Hwy. 1 along the rugged Sonoma County coast.

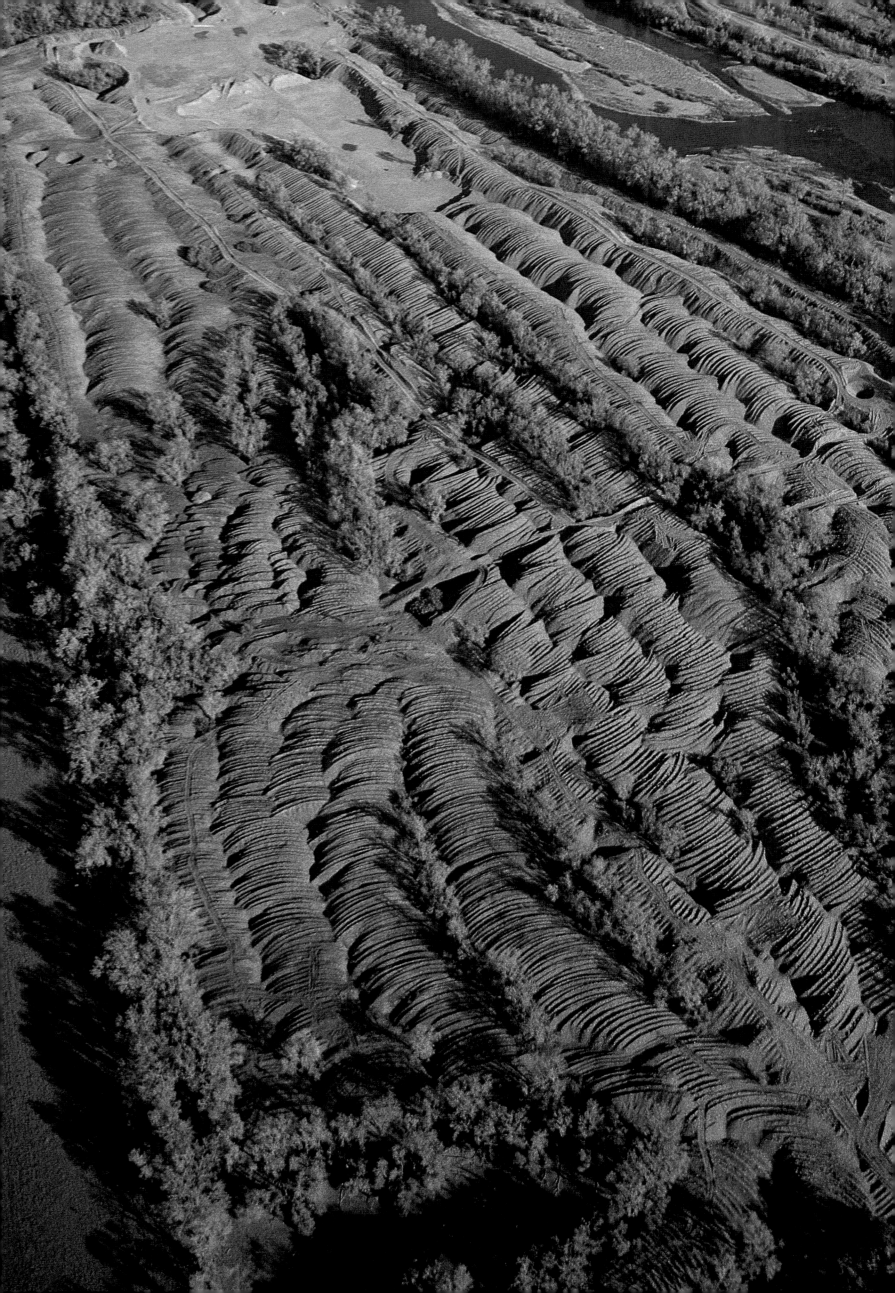

THE GOLD COUNTRY AND SACRAMENTO

Like the Valley of the Po in northern Italy, the Sacramento Valley and the Mother Lode stood as the matrix of trade, transportation, and inland settlement during the first two decades of American California. American mountain men and Hudson's Bay trappers roamed the region in the 1820s and 1830s. In 1839 a German Swiss by the name of Johann Augustus Sutter, a Mexican citizen, acquired a land grant from the Mexican government, centered on the junction of the Sacramento and American rivers. Sutter spent the 1840s transforming New Helvetia, as he called his establishment, into a European-style barony, complete with Miwok and Maidu serfs. It featured a fortified block house

Left: Patterned dredge trailings near the Feather River south of Oroville leave evidence of the search for gold. *Above:* The capitol in Sacramento directs a state that is an empire unto itself.

*F*or the forty-niners, the Sierra Nevada
was at once an arduous barrier and a
source of riches. After the discovery
of gold in 1848, wagon-train traffic
across the Emigrant Trail peaked to an
intensity lasting through the mid-1850s.

on the banks of the Sacramento River with 30-inch-
thick adobe walls and a cannon purchased from the
Russians at Fort Ross.

Sutter's Fort stood as the logical destination of
the emigrant wagon trains. Here the emigrants rested
and were resupplied before continuing their journeys.
Hordes of gold-seekers also squatted on Sutter's property and built a city called Sacramento around the
site of his fort, which is today a restored state historical monument.

Sutter's vision was partially fulfilled in the city of
Sacramento, since 1854 the state capital. Erected

hastily on the banks of the volatile and unleveed
Sacramento River, which overflowed three times
between 1849 and 1853, Sacramento rapidly became
the second city of California after San Francisco.
Five Sacramentans—Theodore Judah, Leland
Stanford, Mark Hopkins, Charles Crocker, and
Collis Huntington—organized the Central Pacific
Railroad in 1861, with the goal of building a railroad
across the Sierra Nevada. Judah died in 1863, but
the Big Four, as history remembers them, stuck to
their program. Thanks to the heroic labor and engineering skills of Chinese construction crews, the rails

of the Central Pacific met the rails of the Union Pacific at Promontory Point, Utah, on May 10, 1869, and the continental United States stood linked by one continuous route. Sacramento then became the major railroad terminus and departure point for transcontinental railroad traffic, a version of the role it had played for the wagon trains.

By that time the state government was near to completing the ornate neoclassical white-wedding-cake capitol, under construction between 1861 and 1874. Set in the center of a 33-acre park around which have grown up some four generations of gov-

ernment buildings, the capitol still manages to exude the breezy optimism of the High Provincial era, 1860–90, when California stood so unsettled and full of promise.

It has taken Sacramento more than a hundred years to fit comfortably into its capital city role. For most of the 19th century, the city reverted between legislative sessions into the sleepy repose of just another farm town in the interior, inhumanly hot in the summer months. Not until the 1950s did Sacramento begin to metropolitanize. Today it is the center of a million-plus suburban region, which includes the nearby university town of Davis, a tree-shaded enclave praised for its quality of life.

In a happy evolution, the Mother Lode of the 1850s has become a summer and skiing resort in the late 20th century. The resort region begins at the crest of the Emigrant Trail—at Lake Tahoe in the counties of Placer and El Dorado, with one-third of its shoreline lying in Nevada. Visiting Lake Tahoe in the early 1860s, Mark Twain claimed that the scenery and pure mountain air could restore an Egyptian mummy to life.

*P*lacerville, on U.S. 50 in El Dorado County, sustains the town plan of its frontier days. Buildings from the mining era still stand, and like many of the towns in this area, Placerville abounds in gold rush memorabilia.

As the lumber industry declined in the late 19th century, Lake Tahoe emerged as a resort for the San Francisco Bay Area. With travel to the Tahoe area primarily by train, the mountain region remained undeveloped and exclusive through the 1930s. The 1950s witnessed the construction of Interstate 80 up from Sacramento, together with a ski boom which motivated thousands to head into the mountains in wintertime. Squaw Valley, overlooking Lake Tahoe, emerged as an important resort destination and served as the site of the 1960 Winter Olympics. The shores of the lake grew dense with condominium developments, and by the early 1970s Lake Tahoe, like Yosemite Valley to the south, suffered intermittently from smog.

Meanwhile the gold rush communities on the western slope of the Sierra Nevada—Oroville, Downieville, Nevada City, Grass Valley, Auburn, Placerville, and the smaller communities of Rough and Ready, Georgetown, Coloma (where the rush

began), and Dutch Flat—were also being discovered, but in a more environmentally benevolent manner. With an excellent highway system in place, these Sierran foothill towns were by the 1980s a string of refurbished communities, their 19th-century red brick buildings recycled as hotels, restaurants, little theaters, boutiques, and wine shops.

In the Sierra foothills, the Northern California lifestyle perhaps achieves its most complete expression; for here is at once wilderness and civility, the outdoor life and indoor sophistication. No wonder this region has experienced a massive influx of permanent settlers. As the San Francisco Bay Area became increasingly crowded and complex to negotiate, and Sacramento itself became a big city, the venerable townships that came into being during the gold rush were once again called to the service of the California dream.

Beneath the rusted tin roofs of downtown Columbia stand brick buildings that survive intact from the gold rush era. The Methodist church, opposite the balconied hotel on Main Street (note the modern swimming pool), has been in use since 1852. Columbia was far from any river, and mining was dry and very difficult. In the spring of 1851 more than 200 men dug a ditch into the area from a remote river so that Columbia could use water in processing its gold-rich topsoil.

Following pages
The Sacramento and the San Joaquin rivers flow together in the delta lands east of Suisun Bay. Here marshes, bogs, and tule swamps are laced together by canals and levees used in flood control.

A narrow separation of Church and State: Blessed Sacrament Cathedral and the state capitol building raise domes to God and Country in the Sacramento twilight.

In the last twenty years Sacramento has nearly tripled its population. Housing developments prosper, such as this one on the eastern side of the city. Plentiful housing, in turn, prompts more companies to relocate to Sacramento. As a sure sign of civic maturity, the city now has a no-growth movement fueled by fears that its much-praised quality of life cannot be sustained amidst headlong expansion.

Thus far, the rolling hills outside Vacaville, in Solano County, have been preserved from suburbanization. Vacaville is onion country, and at certain times of the year the fragrance of fresh onions fills the surrounding area. Hills such as these bespeak California, north or south, simultaneously communicating an ambience of austerity, bleakness even, and friendliness. The *Californios* found these hills excellent for cattle grazing. Don Manuel Vaca, after whom Vacaville was named, deeded the necessary portion of his Rancho los Putos in 1850 to make space for the town. Were the don to return today, he would find the lands outside his city as bare as the day he first drove his longhorn cattle onto the open plain.

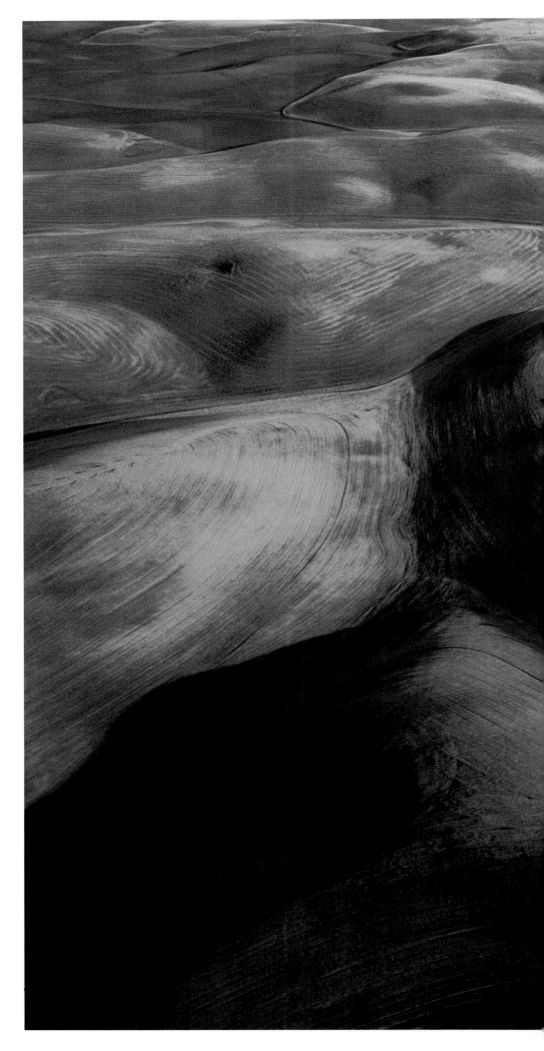

A glint in the gravel was noticed on the South Fork of the American River on January 24, 1848. One hundred and forty years after the gold rush began, Coloma, on Rt. 49 in El Dorado County, is a quiet mountain town in which the state maintains a historical park memorializing the discovery.

*D*ownieville, on Rt. 49 on the North
Fork of the Yuba River, was named
after William Downie, who brought a
mining party to the area in 1849. By
1851 more than 5,000 miners had
flocked to the region to try their luck.

Following pages
*I*ce transforms the shores of Prosser
Creek Reservoir into a study of negative
space. Prosser Creek, near Donner Pass,
is one of many Sierran reservoirs that
store snowmelt water for California's
lowlands.

I-80 crosses the Sierra through Donner Pass just north of Tahoe. The Donner Party (for whom the pass is named) was tragically stranded here in the winter of 1846.

*S*erene in a winter stillness, Lake Tahoe lies tucked between the abrupt slopes of the Sierra Nevada and the Carson Range, which rise over 4,000 feet above the lake. Twenty-two miles long and twelve miles wide, the lake is a famous year-round resort.

*E*merald Bay is among the most beautiful of the many inlets, coves, and bays lining the shore of Lake Tahoe. Set aside as a state park, Emerald Bay retains the wild grandeur threatened by the area's heavily used resorts. Miles of state forests and protected wilderness further maintain the ecological balance of the region.

THE NATURAL NORTH

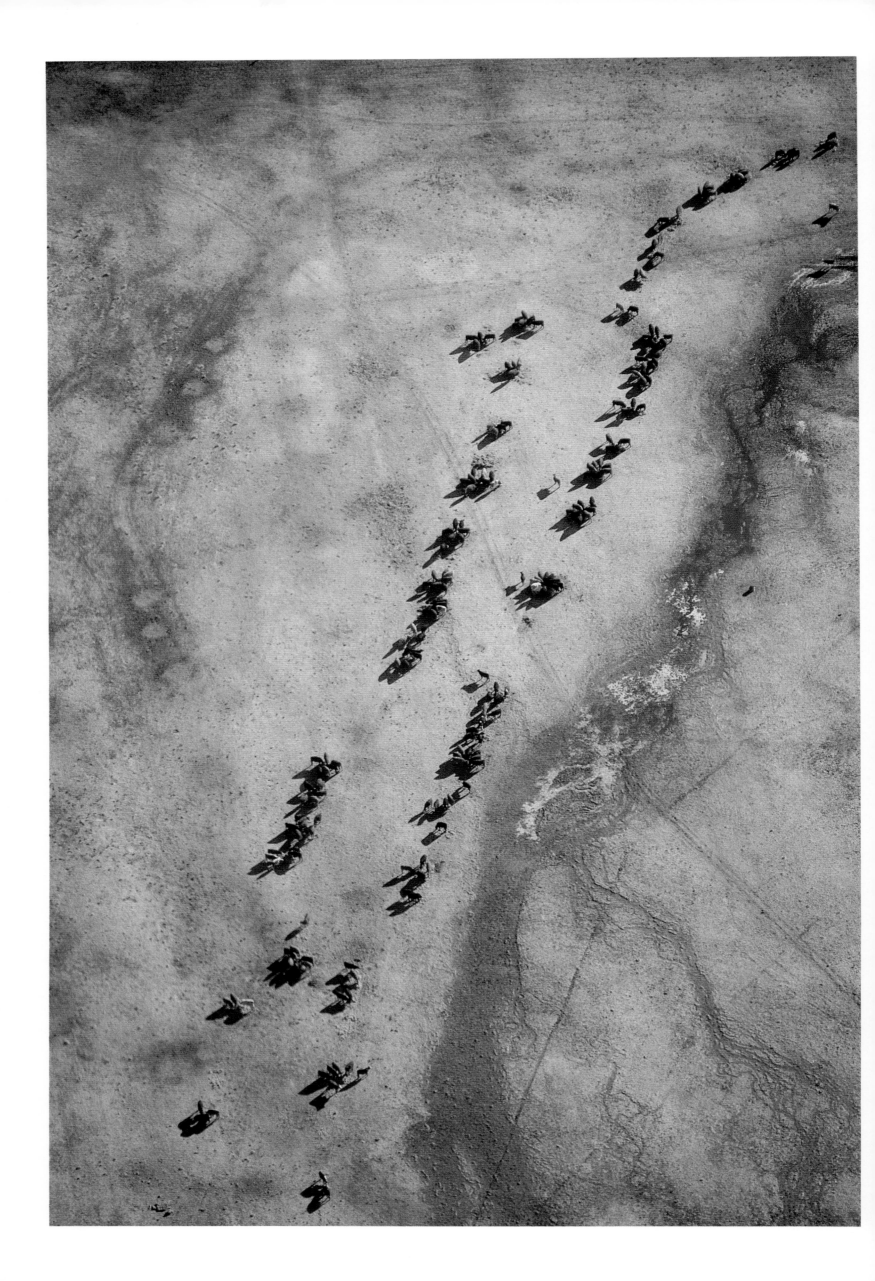

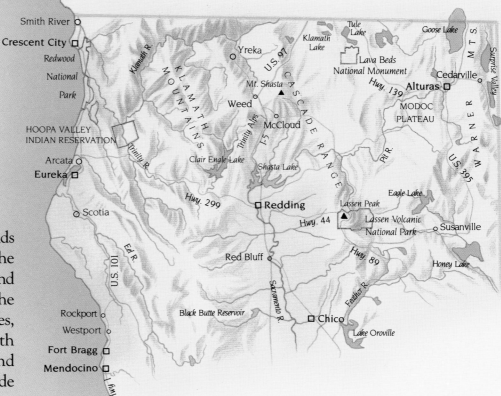

The Natural North extends across the top tier of the state. Mountains, rivers, and man-made lakes dominate the region. Two great mountain ranges, the glacially formed Klamath Mountains in the northwest and the volcanically formed Cascade Range in the center, determine the topography.

The Klamath, the Trinity, the Eel, the Sacramento, the Pit, and the Feather are the most conspicuous rivers in the Natural North, yet the Mattole, the Scott, the Salmon, the Mad, the Van Duzen, the McCloud, and the Noyo play important roles in their respective sectors. Man-made lakes such as Clair Engle, Shasta, Almanor, and Oroville form a major irrigation and hydroelectric network supplying the entire state, and are major destination points in the tourist and vacation economy. Clear Lake, Lake Pillsbury, Black Butte Lake, Lake Shastina, Lower Klamath Lake, Eagle Lake, and Goose Lake, which extends into Oregon, are also important reservoirs and recreational areas.

The redwood tree (*Sequoia sempervirens*) is the most conspicuous inhabitant of the Natural North—a source of lumber in the 19th century, a major tourist attraction in the 20th. Thanks to conservation efforts begun by the Save-the-Redwoods League in 1918, this ancient tree, capable of living 2,000 years and reaching heights of 300 feet, has been guaranteed permanence along the Natural North coastline.

Arcata and Eureka on the coast, together with the plateau town of Yreka in the interior, constitute the urban centers of the Natural North. There are also a number of smaller population centers—Fort Bragg and Crescent City on the western side; Burney, Weed, and McCloud in the center; and Alturas and Susanville in the east. Here a small-city to small-town to village lifestyle is possible.

With the exception of the coast, the Natural North is dramatically underpopulated, much of it being allocated to state or federal parks, forest preserves, or privately held timberland. As the watershed of California, the Natural North catches and holds over two-thirds of the rain or snow falling each year on the state. With the population of California increasing by fifteen, perhaps twenty million through the first quarter of the 21st century, it is likely that the Natural North will increase in population as well, with Eureka, Crescent City, and Redding absorbing much of the growth. For this to happen, however, the fishing, lumber, and public-sector economy of the Natural North will have to be diversified and expanded in new directions that have not yet clarified themselves.

Perhaps a more important destiny awaits the Natural North, that of remaining a wilderness watershed, the lungs and circulatory system of the increasingly crowded southern and central tiers. From this perspective, the Natural North remains the Maine and Vermont of California—its continuing connection with the primeval wilderness that was California through the 19th century.

A frosty winter morning and ranchers hand-feed their cattle in Lassen County.

Previous pages
Fog creeps over Russian Gulch in Redwood National Park.

THE REDWOOD EMPIRE

The North Coast resembles Big Sur as experienced and presented by the poet Robinson Jeffers: a place that encourages human beings to bestill themselves, look within, and reflect. The North Coast is also alive with the realities and metaphors of the lumber and fishing industries which first settled this area in the 19th century.

Founded in 1857 as a military post guarding the Mendocino Indian Reservation, Fort Bragg grew up as the industrial center for the Union Lumber Company sawmill operation. While the lumbering era lasted in its unregulated form, it was ferocious. Down in San Francisco, entire districts such as the Western Addition were constructed with row upon row of Victorian homes similar to the Carson House in Eureka, in which every detail was fashioned from prime redwood.

Left: The Trinity Alps are as magnificent as their European namesakes. *Above:* Mount Shasta, elevation 14,162 feet, is a solitary giant of volcanic origin.

South of Fort Bragg at Noyo, Alexander Wentworth Macpherson carved out a way of life for himself that is still remembered in local tradition. Born in Inverness, Scotland, in 1824, Macpherson was a Pacific Rim man 160 years before the term pushed itself into the California consciousness. Between 1849 and 1853, he sailed to Australia from San Francisco on business and visited a number of major Pacific Rim cities in the course of his return.

In a complicated financial arrangement, Macpherson oversaw in 1854 the construction of a sawmill at Albion, south of Mendocino. Shortly thereafter, he expanded his operation north to Noyo. A glass-plate negative made by the great California photographer Carleton Watkins shows the Noyo sawmill in the year 1863 as a flourishing industrial operation. Macpherson built an elegant home on a hill for his wife, Petrita Gonzales, and their four children. He lived there in opulence and taste.

Macpherson's lavish hospitality foreshadowed the current economy of the North Coast as a tourist destination point. The entire region between Fort Bragg and Jenner in northern Sonoma County, where the Russian River runs into the sea, is today flourishing with hostelries of every description.

Yet despite this hostelry and restaurant culture, Fort Bragg, Noyo, and Albion still preserve the feel and, to a certain extent, the reality of the founding industry of this region. Great stocks or rafts of logs still await cutting as they did in the days of Alexander Wentworth Macpherson.

The Klamath Indians once roamed these forests, leaving their name to the mountains, a river, and a lake. The Hoopa Indians now fish the Klamath River.

The Louisiana-Pacific lumbermill sits on the Samoa Peninsula, with Eureka in the background. Here lumber is cut from redwood and fir trees, particle board is manufactured, and wood pulp is mixed for shipment to paper makers.

The Eel River is one of several whitewater rivers in Northern California targeted for protection by environmentalists.

*T*oday a private club, the Carson Mansion in Eureka symbolizes the prosperity brought to the largest city of the Natural North by the lumber industry.

*L*ogging and fishing are the most important industries for the residents of Fairhaven. The lifestyle of the North Coast resembles that of Maine— only, as columnist Jimmy Breslin once pointed out, the ocean is on the wrong side.

Ocean fog skims across mysterious cliffs of Battery Point at the edge of Crescent City's harbor. In 1865 a steamer, the *Brother Jonathan*, went down in the rocky shallows with 200 passengers on board. Tragedy visited these waters again in 1964 when a tidal wave caused by the Alaskan earthquake ripped ashore, destroying much of Crescent City.

Logs await processing at the Pacific Lumber Company in Scotia, the largest redwood mill in the world. Computers are used to manage the input, output, and precision cutting of the logs.

At Cape Vizcaino, in Mendocino County, sea fog glides through the giant redwood trees (*Sequoia sempervirens*) like a mysterious presence seeking out secret places. The fog brings the forest's only source of water during the dry summer months.

159

A ranch house near Eureka suggests
the New England origins of so many
pioneers in the Natural North.
Mendocino and parts of Fort Bragg
and Eureka are Yankee picturesque
in a Vermont sort of way.

Previous pages
Hwy. 1 skirts the edge of the tiny
village of Westport before turning
inland. A few miles north of here,
in an area known as the Lost Coast,
the continent's edge becomes too
precipitous and rocky for human
habitation.

*H*istory, but not the fog, has forgotten so many places on the Mendocino coast. Numerous small communities— Usal, Rockport, Noyo, Albion, Navarro, among others—sprang up during the glory days of the lumber industry. Today some small cash-crops, or an odd job here and there, allow for a life among the redwoods, pines, and cypresses that thrive in the sunshine and sea fog.

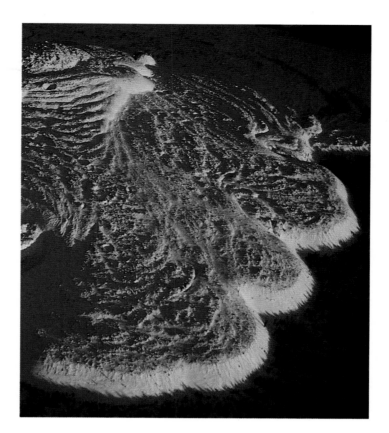

THE MODOC PLATEAU

Averaging more than 4,000 feet in elevation, the geologically spectacular Modoc Plateau represents an intrusion of the Great Basin into the northeastern sector of the Natural North, extending westward to the Cascade Range. With the exception of the deserts to the south, no portion of California is more sparsely settled than this volcanic region, with under three persons per square mile. North of Susanville, there are only a few small towns. Most of Modoc and Lassen counties, in fact, which account for most of the plateau, are taken up with national forests.

On the western edge of the plateau, extending into Siskiyou County, are the Modoc Lava Beds. To the southwest rises the most described and painted peak in all of California, Mount Shasta, in southern Siskiyou County. Created by both volcanic and glacial action, Mount Shasta abruptly ascends from

Left: A cloud ring encircles the snowy summit of Mount Shasta. *Above:* The Native Americans of northeastern California called their home the Amblu-Kai, or fiery plateau.

its surrounding plain "lonely as God and white as a winter moon," as the poet Joaquin Miller described this 14,162-feet montane apparition.

Between 1872 and 1873, the Modoc War, the single costliest campaign of the Indian Wars—83 whites and seventeen Indians dead, a half-million dollars spent—raged through the lava beds near the Oregon border in Siskiyou County. In 1869 the Modocs had been removed from their ancestral lands in the lava regions and placed on a reservation in Oregon. The Modocs disliked the reservation and its Indian agent. They loathed the Klamath Indians, hereditary enemies with whom they were forced to live. In 1872 a party of Modocs headed south, determined to live in the lands of their ancestors. Led by the brilliant tactician Captain Jack Kientepoos,

fewer than a hundred Modocs held off more than a thousand Army regulars, together with their civilian and Indian auxiliaries, through superior marksmanship and a skilled guerrilla use of the outcroppings, caves, cliffs, trenches, and backtrails of the lava beds.

The Modocs eventually surrendered on the promise that they would be treated as prisoners of war. Captain Jack and three other Modocs were later tried, convicted, and hanged at Fort Klamath for shooting down unarmed Brigadier General Edward Canby and Dr. Eleazer Thomas as they parleyed under a flag of truce. Canby thus became the only Army general to lose his life in the Indian Wars. Had Captain Jack not been goaded into the killings in the mistaken belief that the soldiers would go away when their general was dead, he might have lived

Below: The sagebrush-covered basin and range country that begins here in Surprise Valley near Cedarville typifies the ranch country of most of the western United States. *Right:* A view of the Warner Mountains from the town of Alturas.

out his life on the Kansas reservation to which the rest of the Modocs were sent—a legendary figure, the Sitting Bull, Geronimo, or even Cochise of the Natural North.

But then again: what about all those young troopers lying dead in the lava beds, victims of a mis-guided Indian policy? The very fact that General Canby had initially objected to Army orders to bring the Modocs back to the Oregon reservation by force, and was shot down while trying to negotiate a peaceful settlement, lent further tragedy to the Modoc War.

The philosopher Josiah Royce claimed that the California landscape was characterized by grandeur and clear delineations. This view of the geometric farmlands at Newell, Modoc County, leading to Mount Shasta on the horizon, supports his theory.

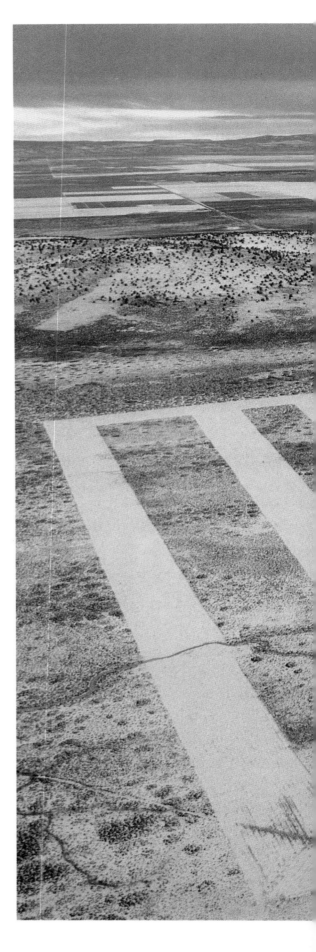

*I*n the harsh climate of the Modoc Plateau, summer heat can exceed 100 degrees, while winter brings snow and sub-zero temperatures. Plowed alfalfa fields (*far right*) form a grid that adds scale to the landscape. Extensive marshes, such as this frozen one (*right*), provide habitat for thousands of water fowl and hunting grounds for the plateau's substantial bald eagle population. A view of ranches in Surprise Valley (*above*) exposes a delicate tracery of trails, roads, and hedgerows which fade into the distant Warner Mountains.

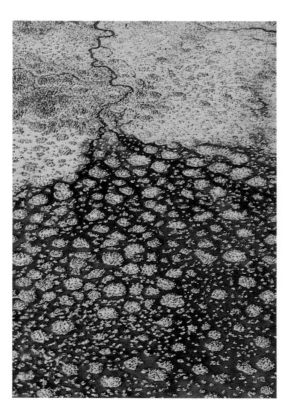

*I*n Surprise Valley, cattle continue to return to a ranch long abandoned to the harsh elements of the high country.

*T*he warmth of a natural hot springs in Surprise Valley attracts cattle from the frozen plain. The geothermal activity of the Modoc Plateau creates many such hot springs.

War casts a subtle shadow over
the Modoc. During World War II,
thousands of Japanese Americans were
removed to an internment camp near
Newell. Though this tattered building
is all that remains of the physical place,
the memory of U.S. citizens being
forcibly relocated by the government
remains a disturbing legacy. *Right:* The
Army stores munitions in these somber
bunkers at the Sierra Depot in the
Honey Lake Valley.

A Yokut Indian legend tells that Hawk made the eastern mountains and Crow the western. They built the mountains up with dirt carried in their beaks, and eventually they met here at Mount Shasta. Hawk discovered that Crow's mountains were much higher than his own because Crow had been cheating. Hawk promptly swapped the mountains, and that is why the Sierra Nevada is so much higher than the Coast Range.

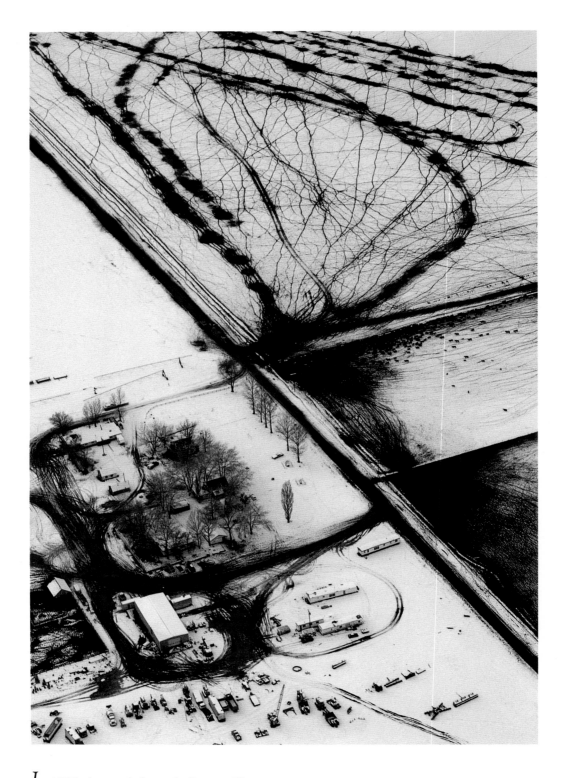

In 1922 the road through Coyote Flat, on the Madeline Plains in Lassen County, was paved. Once known as the Hyampon Trail, the road has been in use since the 1860s. Madeline Plains is ranch country: flat, remote, and buried in snow during the winter months when cattle come to feed. Their trails leave traces against the wide horizon.

In Modoc County hay and hungry cattle form an X against the Surprise Valley snow.

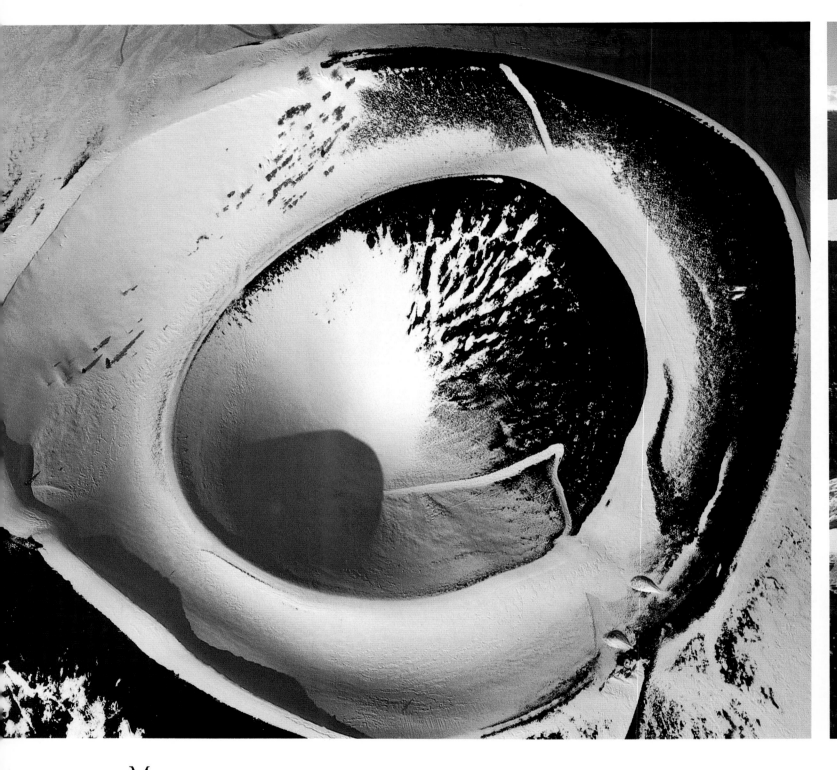

Mount Tehama in Lassen Volcanic National Park was once an active volcano. This cinder cone is all that remains—a dramatic suggestion of the fiery convulsions that shaped the Modoc Plateau.

*L*assen Peak, elevation 10,457 feet, looms above a volcanic landscape of cinder cones and lava beds whitened by snow. Lassen erupted most recently in 1921 and is the sole remaining active volcano in California.

THE INVENTED GARDEN

The Latin verb *invenire* means to come upon, to discover that which is already there. Its English derivative *invent* suggests the creation of a new entity. The concept of the Invented Garden includes both notions. The garden was always there in the interior of California, but it also had to be invented through irrigation projects of heroic magnitude.

The Invented Garden begins with the Inland Empire of the South, embracing the irrigated agricultural regions of Riverside, San Bernardino, and Imperial counties. It then leaps across the Tehachapi Range into the valley of the San Joaquin and moves northward through the valley of the Sacramento until it meets the Natural North.

Interstate 5 and State Highway 99 link the major urban centers of the Invented Garden, beginning with Redding in the north and proceeding south through or by Red Bluff, Chico, Sacramento, Stockton, Modesto, Merced, Fresno, and Bakersfield. South of the Tehachapis the Invented Garden is served by Interstates 10, 40, and 15. Its urban centers are San Bernardino, Riverside, Redlands, Thousand Palms, Indio, Coachella, Brawley, El Centro, and Imperial. Greater Palm Springs represents the Invented Garden as desert resort.

Touring the as-of-yet Uninvented Garden in 1859, New York *Tribune* editor Horace Greeley wondered where all the people were. Not until the 1870s does one encounter the systematic settlement of the Central Valley. Land, water, and an available labor force have spurred the Invented Garden toward its present growth. The cities of the Invented Garden are attracting more and more people from the coast.

The Invented Garden is also in the process of entering the global economy. Spain and Portugal, for example, are wreaking havoc on the raisin industry of Fresno. Mexico might have problems with its oil industry, but its cauliflower, broccoli, and tomatoes are giving nightmares to California farmers faced with labor costs that can soar ten or more times higher than those to the south. The Invented Garden today faces the necessity to key itself competitively to world markets and to world competition.

The Invented Garden remains American home country, sophisticated enough to be interesting, but staying closer than the polyglot culture of the coast to American things: the porch, county fairs, church socials, nights spent in the backyard over corn on the cob, baked potatoes, and hamburgers spread out on a picnic table. With its vast fields and emerging cities, its interplay of agribusiness and county fairs, its pickup trucks and BMWs, its truck stops and college campuses, the Invented Garden now claims equal partnership with the other Californias.

*F*lowing southwest from the Sierra Nevada, the Kings River passes through the counties of Fresno and Kings.

Previous pages

*D*ue to an abundance of water, the Central Valley has become a long, green garden stretching 450 miles down the center of the state.

185

THE CENTRAL VALLEY

The aspect of the California landscape that most impressed Josiah Royce, native son and philosopher, was its clarity. In California, Royce observed, the dominant topographies—mountain, valley, flatland, desert, and seacoast—do not edge into each other as a matter of subtle transition. They face each other boldly, dramatically, clearly. In the Central Valley, the great flatlands are confronted, east and west, by the clearly determined, visually accessible Sierra Nevada and coast mountain ranges.

In general, then, the landscape of the Invented Garden is not intimate but heroic, even abstract. Interstates 80 and 5 move through landscapes that extend in every direction toward distant mountain ranges. And yet the signs of irrigation and agriculture are everywhere—canals, silos, orchards, and planted fields as far as the eye can see—engendering an atmosphere of remote human power, as if an absent race of giants had planted this great garden, then

Left: The San Joaquin Valley—an orderly arrangement of roads, fields, houses, and cypress groves. *Above:* Spring planting commences in a field near Orland.

stole away into the mountains. But it was men and women, Californians, not legendary giants, who invented the garden.

The Central Valley is the single richest agricultural region in the world. Its fifteen million acres represent one-sixth of the irrigated cropland in the United States. Fully a quarter of what America eats—its fruits, vegetables, cereals, poultry, and meats—has Central Valley origins.

It began with wheat, the first bonanza crop of the upper Central Valley. By 1880 wheat grower Hugh James Glenn, a sometime dentist from Missouri, was producing a half-million bushels per year on his Colusa County ranch, which employed up to 600 at harvest time. Wheat baron Isaac Friedlander shipped three-quarters of his harvests to England and Europe in ships he owned or leased. By 1889 California was shipping twenty million bushels abroad each year from gigantic grain depots at Port Costa on the eastern side of San Francisco Bay.

Irrigation and the refrigerated freight car diversified the wheat economy of the Central Valley. Wheat was a dry crop. With water, just about everything could be grown. Between 1880 and 1920 California fashioned itself into an agricultural empire. Central Valley ranchers favored fruit and nut crops that ripened before the long hot summer. Peaches and pear trees proved ideal and were planted by the tens of thousands. By 1920 Fresno County was producing half of the world's raisins. Other hot-weather crops, figs and melons especially, flourished on the flat irrigated fields, as did nectarines, prunes, walnuts, almonds, tomatoes, carrots, and the non-edible but important crop of cotton.

Equally important is the oil and natural gas crop of the Central Valley. Since the 1860s oil has been drilled in the San Joaquin. Today's megagiants such as Chevron and Unocal, formerly Standard and Union, have extensive San Joaquin Valley origins.

To harvest 200 separate crops maturing at various seasons, to drill for oil and natural gas, takes work, plenty of it, and that means working men and women. The labor history of California is concerned

in great part with the structured difficulties, the built-in inequities, of what social commentator Carey McWilliams described as "factories in the fields." Agricultural labor is difficult: it succeeds only through bent backs, aching muscles, long hours under the unforgiving Central Valley sun. It is also by its very nature seasonal. Thus there has always been a high degree of labor strife in the Central Valley.

And yet, successive generations of immigrants have experienced social mobility after coming to the Central Valley as agricultural laborers. Chinese, Japanese, East Indian, Filipino, Anglo-American migrants from the Dust Bowl, black Americans from the South: all have begun their California sojourn bent over the harvest under the remorseless sun.

The most consistent source of field labor has been Mexican. Beginning with World War II, large numbers of Mexicans were brought to the Central Valley under the Bracero program. Others came illegally. In time, others were born in the United States to farm-labor families. In the 1960s the National Farm Workers Union began to organize the previously unorganizable, and a new slogan, *huelga* (strike), and a new national leader, Cesar Chavez, entered the American consciousness.

The Central Valley can be considered a California unto itself, complete with cities and towns, industrial and recreational areas, set amidst the all-pervasive realities of agribusiness. Central Valley towns— Bakersfield, Fresno, Merced, Modesto, Marysville,

A ship wends its way through the valley toward the inland deepwater port of Stockton. The cities of this region, such as Stockton on the San Joaquin River and Redding on the Sacramento River to the north, are working cities, more matter-of-fact than picturesque.

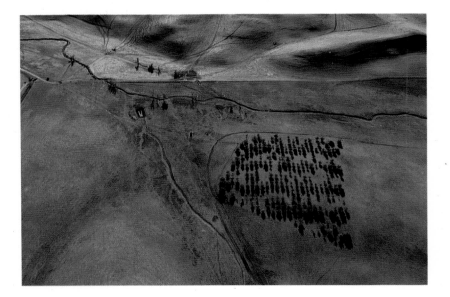

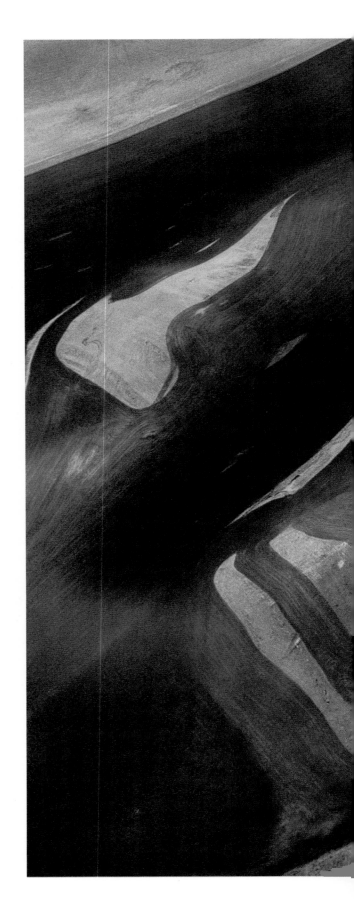

Chico, Redding, and their smaller counterparts—are in a transitional state.

Today, each of the valley towns, while discernibly different in texture and tone from the coastal cities, boasts such amenities as college campuses, shopping centers, bookstores, and good restaurants. The county fairs of the Central Valley are preeminent festivals. As the gateway to Yosemite, the Central Valley sustains its own resort and recreational culture at such places as Shaver Lake, Bass Lake, and the ski country around Yosemite itself.

Valley people are Californians of their own sort. Life in the valley is a little more direct, a little less complicated, perhaps, than on the coast. Even now, however, University of California campuses are being planned for the area, the Fresno airport is constantly expanding, and some of the raw, unplanned quality is disappearing from the peripheries of the major cities. As land costs continue to soar on the coast, a more diversified population can be expected to in-migrate.

But for the time being, the Central Valley still communicates a fundamental yet often forgotten fact: for all its social complexity, California is the West and retains in its social texture and value system the simplicities, frank appetites, and elemental struggles of its frontier heritage.

The rich, rolling earth of the Sacramento Valley has yielded abundant fruit and wheat crops. The wheat first grown in this area by pioneer John Bidwell was judged the finest grain in the world at the Paris International Exposition of 1878.

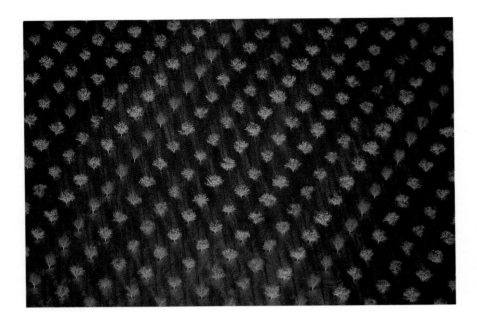

*E*tched against pastures bearing the last blush of spring green, an orchard near Bakersfield appears like writing in a foreign alphabet. Stone fruits (peaches, plums, cherries) were the first choice of valley farmers, who planted over three million peach trees in the 1890s alone.

*C*alifornia poppies (*Eschscholztia californica*) tint an arid hillside with a wash of saffron. As the official state flower, California poppies are protected in this reserve near Tehachapi Pass. They are still the most common flower in the countryside and are often found growing in the cracks of city sidewalks.

*I*n the beginning and always was the land. From the land, the first and last premise of the California experience, Californians sought with increasing success to feed themselves, then the nation, and then the world. In 1879 agriculture succeeded mining as the primary industry of the state—a hegemony that has lasted over one hundred years.

*I*n Modesto, a well-known wine company stores wine for the nation. Irrigation pipes cut a diagonal pattern across nearby fields.

*S*outh Korea, ironically, is a major buyer of California rice. The grain's delicate presence on the landscape adds a note of antiquity to this field near Merced.

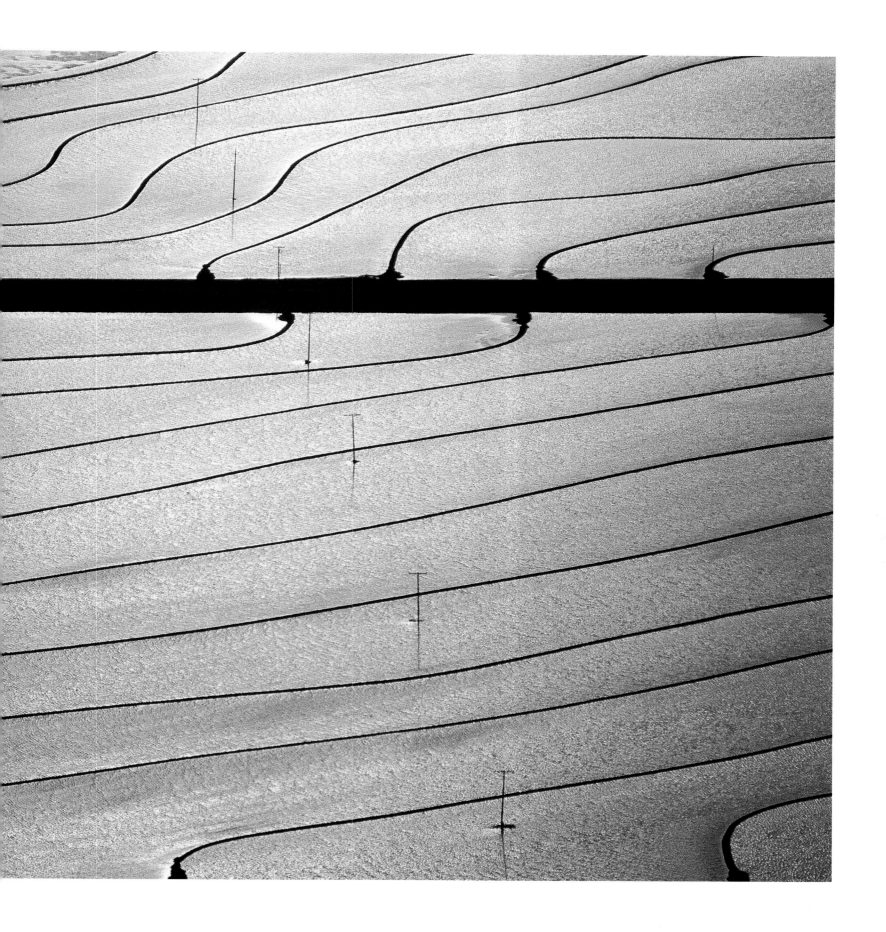

As the suburbs crawl eastward from
Los Angeles, the citrus orchards that
were once common in Riverside County
are reappearing in the north near
Fresno. Fed by the waters of the San
Joaquin River, orange groves such as
these account for a large part of the
263,000 acres of land devoted to citrus
growing in California. Peaches, plums,
lemons, and grapes are also grown in
the Fresno area.

*B*etween 1895 and 1920 a number of major oil fields were discovered on the eastern side of the San Joaquin Valley. One gusher, Lakeview Number One, yielded ten million barrels of oil. The oil region centers around the town of Taft, named after the president.

The Air Museum at Castle Air Force Base, near Merced, testifies to the major role California has played in the design and manufacture of military aircraft and the training of flight crews. During World War II thousands of pilots, navigators, bombardiers, aerial gunners, maintenance crews, and other personnel received their training at California bases, many of them in the Central Valley.

Redding marks the northern boundary
of the Central Valley. Unlike most
valley towns, Redding's proximity to
Mount Shasta, the Trinity Alps, and
Shasta Lake make it a resort and
vacation center.

Oroville Dam, 770 feet high, confines the waters of the Feather River in Lake Oroville. South of the lake, the Feather River was once the site of rich gold fields. Today the lake's carefully controlled waters irrigate the fields of the Sacramento Valley.

An age-old agricultural technique of
Native Americans for clearing brush,
burning is used today on grass-seed
fields in the Central Valley to rid the
soil of unwanted weeds and pests.

A dirt road leads through a canyon in
the coastal hills near King City. Brown
in the summer, these hills will take on
an emerald-velvet lushness after the
rains come in winter.

IRRIGATION

When it comes to the distribution of water, nature has issued California a special challenge. Two-thirds of all precipitation falls in the northern tier of the state; two-thirds of the population lives in Southern California. For nearly 100 years, California has been creating a statewide system designed to carry water from where it is to where it is needed.

The city of Los Angeles completed an aqueduct from the Owens River in the southeastern Sierra as early as 1913. In 1941 the waters of the Colorado River were brought to the desert regions along California's southern border, and in the 1960s San Diego linked itself to the river for its metropolitan water supply. Reaching north for its water, Sacramento takes it from Shasta Lake and Lake Oroville, two artificially created reservoirs. The San Francisco Bay Area draws upon the Mokelumne and Tuolomne rivers in the central Sierra Nevada to the east. The Hetch Hetchy Aqueduct, originating near Yosemite, serves San Francisco and the Peninsula; it was completed in 1934.

Since California's Central Valley contains one-sixth of all the irrigated cropland in the United States, agricultural concerns also affect the state's water divisions. Ever since the early missionaries built *zanjas*, or open ditches, to bring water to mission gardens, irrigation has remained a critical issue.

First planned in the 1930s and completed in the early 1970s, the Central Valley Project incorporates three dams (Shasta, Keswick, and Friant) and five major canals to bring the waters of the Sacramento, McCloud, Pit, and San Joaquin rivers to the farmlands and interior cities of the Golden State. Completed in 1973, the 440-mile Governor Edmund G. Brown California Aqueduct runs down the western side of the San Joaquin Valley, from Tracy to Lake Perris in northwestern Riverside County.

Truly, California has invented itself through water. It was through water-related public works (canals, reservoirs) that the state first envisioned its future. Making these imagined projects a reality has, perhaps more than any other event, defined the face of California today.

Above: The Los Angeles Aqueduct, completed in 1913, carries water to the great southern metropolis. *Left:* Irrigation has made possible the greening of thousands of acres of arid desert lands. *Right:* Parker Dam on the Colorado River creates Lake Havasu.

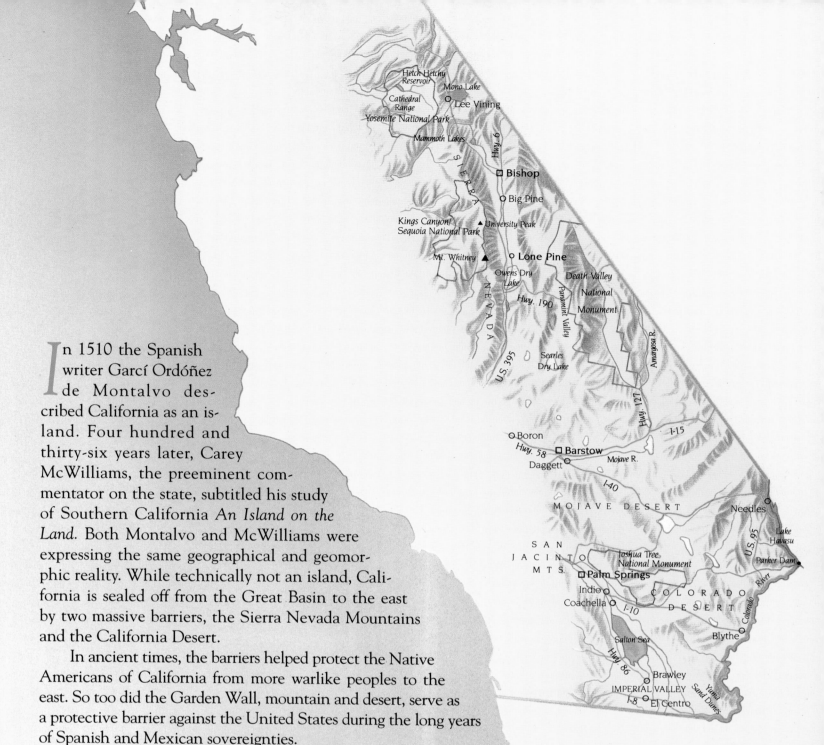

In 1510 the Spanish writer Garcí Ordóñez de Montalvo described California as an island. Four hundred and thirty-six years later, Carey McWilliams, the preeminent commentator on the state, subtitled his study of Southern California *An Island on the Land*. Both Montalvo and McWilliams were expressing the same geographical and geomorphic reality. While technically not an island, California is sealed off from the Great Basin to the east by two massive barriers, the Sierra Nevada Mountains and the California Desert.

In ancient times, the barriers helped protect the Native Americans of California from more warlike peoples to the east. So too did the Garden Wall, mountain and desert, serve as a protective barrier against the United States during the long years of Spanish and Mexican sovereignties.

When Mexican governor Manuel Micheltorena saw Jedediah Smith and his mountain men marching toward Mission San Gabriel on November 27, 1826, he must have intuited the eventual annexation of California by the United States, for Smith and his party had crossed the Mojave Desert and thus completed the first recorded journey from the Missouri River to California. Known as the Old Spanish Trail or Santa Fe Trail, the route pioneered by Smith and his men left Santa Fe for Colorado, crossed southern Utah, then followed the Virgin and Colorado rivers into California via the present-day Needles area.

Kentucky fur trapper William Wolfskill reached Los Angeles in 1831 via the Old Spanish Trail and settled happily in the region as a rancher, among the first of many Americans to infiltrate California via this route. During the gold rush, miners and immigrants preferred to take the sea route via Panama or Nicaragua rather than negotiate the Great Basin and the Sierra Nevada or the desert. The Sierra Nevada succumbed to the Central Pacific Railroad in 1869. The Atchison, Topeka & Santa Fe Railroad completed its line across the Mojave via Needles into Los Angeles in 1885.

While the Garden Wall is today crossed by Interstates 80, 15, 40, and 10, together with a host of state and county secondary roads, the Sierra Nevada and the California Desert still help preserve California's unique climate and, more importantly, preserve California's special sense of location and place.

The Chalfant Valley in Mono County, on the eastern side of the Sierra, is one of many Garden Wall barriers.

Previous pages

In the 1860s geologist Clarence King compared these peaks to the Gothic spires of European cathedrals.

211

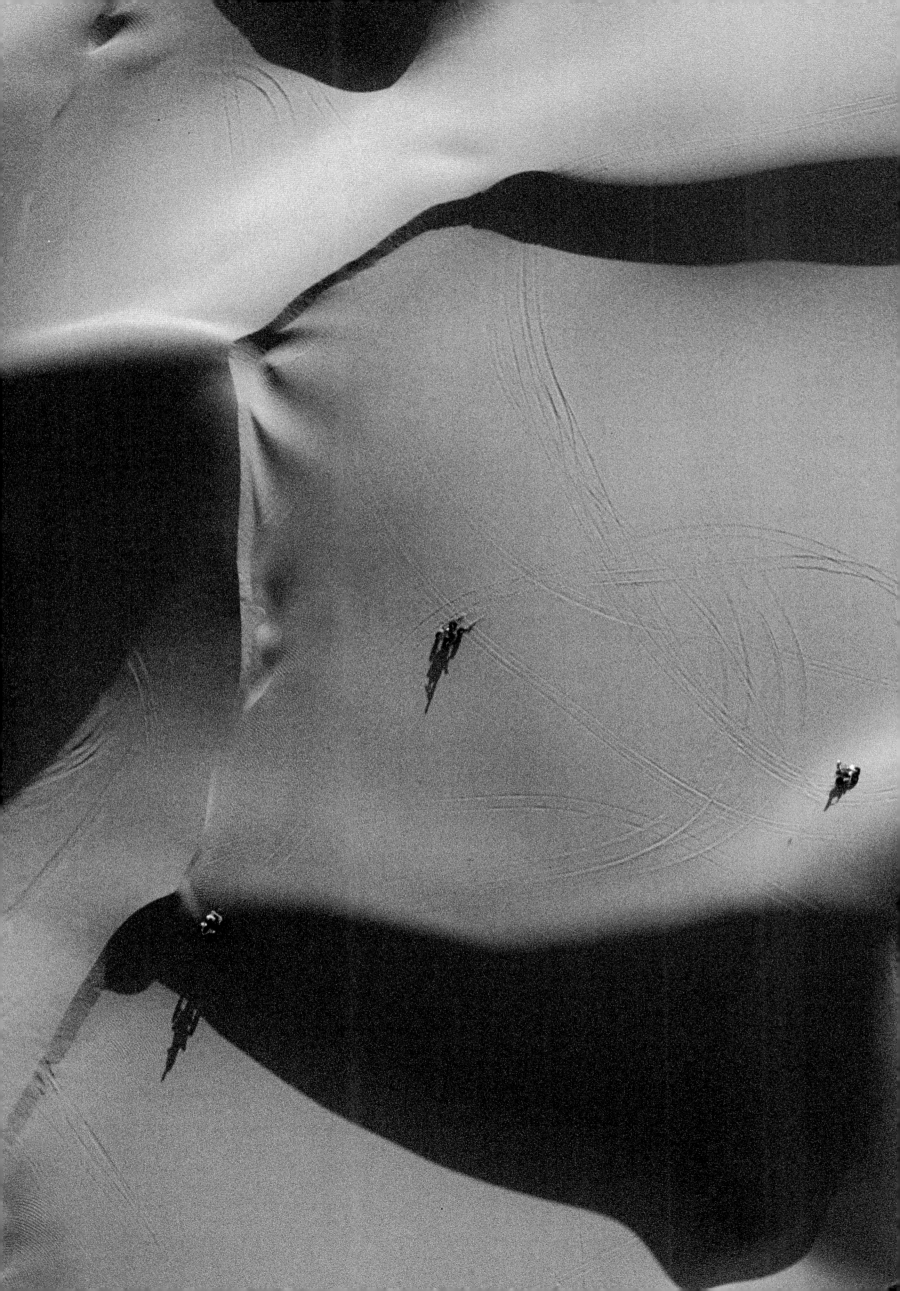

THE MOJAVE AND COLORADO DESERTS

In the American imagination, the desert represents an arena of spiritual renewal and moral regeneration, charged with the biblical memory of the wanderings of the Israelites. The desert is also a trackless and hostile abyss, the very antithesis of the Garden of the West. In many early 19th-century maps, the entire West was designated the Great American Desert, since Americans believed that something like a Sahara covered this region. For Americans traveling overland to California—mountain men Jedediah Smith and James Ohio Pattie, gold-seeker Oliver Merideth Wozencraft, and William Lewis Manly, who led a wagon train across Death Valley in 1849—the desert existed as a formidable, indeed trans-human barrier, a ring of fire sealing California from

Left: On the sand hills off I-8 just west of Yuma, dirt bikers trace ephemeral patterns across the dunes.
Above: Motorboats skim the surface of Lake Havasu.

the rest of the nation. By the 1890s and early 1900s, however, a new generation of Californians—writers George Wharton James, John Van Dyke, and Mary Austin, the painter Maynard Dixon—were finding in the desert a supernal beauty, disciplined and austere, that met their hunger for the sublime as completely as any Sierran peak.

Taken together, the Mojave and the Colorado deserts spread themselves across southeastern California. While the desert is vast and empty, it is also busily put to use. It is, among other things, one of the most important military zones in the country. The Navy maintains a Weapons Testing Center at China Lake. South of China Lake on Highway 395, the Air Force runs the Edwards Flight Test Center. Northeast of Barstow is the Army's Camp Irwin, and south of Camp Irwin off Interstate 40 is the Marine Corps Base of Twentynine Palms.

South of this military corridor are the resort center of Greater Palm Springs, the Joshua Tree National Monument, and the Imperial Valley and Salton Sea. The preemptive presence of military installations has kept the northern tier of the Mojave empty with the exception of the cities of Barstow and Victorville. The southern tier, by contrast, is being increasingly characterized by a built environment running from San Bernardino to Riverside to Greater Palm Springs.

North of the Salton Sea is the Joshua Tree National Monument, which lies between the high Mojave and the low Colorado deserts. In these 850 square miles is preserved the desert environment in its purest possible form. The Colorado River Aqueduct skirts the southwestern edge of the Monument, bringing into Southern California a major portion of its water supply from the mighty Colorado. On the other side of the aqueduct is the Coachella Valley, part of the Colorado Desert that extends east to the Colorado River and south to the Gulf of California. While still agricultural in nature and famous for its date groves, the Coachella Valley is experiencing a building up of its environment from Palm Springs to its west; indeed, the corridor formed by Palm Springs, Cathedral City, Rancho Mirage,

Palm Desert, Indian Wells, and Indio can be considered an emergent metropolitan region of its own—a spectacular resort city, with swimming pools and golf courses in abundance. Fortunately, the Agua Caliente Indians, the original people of this region, have held on to much of their property. The thermal waters which they first discovered and a nearby stand of palm trees provided the name Palm Springs.

South of Palm Springs is Anza-Borrego Desert State Park, which is immediately adjacent to Cleveland National Forest. At this point, the Garden Wall merges back into California del Sur at Ramona on Highway 78, named in honor of the Native American heroine of Helen Hunt Jackson's 1884 novel, *Ramona*, which first broadcast to the rest of America the poetry and romance of this desert region.

*I*ndio, in Riverside County, is the date capital of America. Its annual Date Festival features camel races and date milkshakes. The date palms of Indio, imported at the turn of the century from North Africa and the Middle East, reinforce the town's Mediterranean atmosphere.

The resort city of Palm Springs lies directly below the San Jacinto Mountains, a sea of irrigated green against a dry desert wall.

Palm Springs supports dozens of golf courses—verdant testimony to the ability of money and water to make the desert bloom in greensward and fairways. Retired President Eisenhower and comedian Bob Hope helped make Palm Springs the golf capital of America.

Alluvial fans in Death Valley National Monument unfold where flash floods have left deposits of sand and gravel. Death Valley has the lowest elevation, 282 feet below sea level, in the United States. Ubehebe Crater (*right*), at the park's northern edge, is the scar from an ancient meteor.

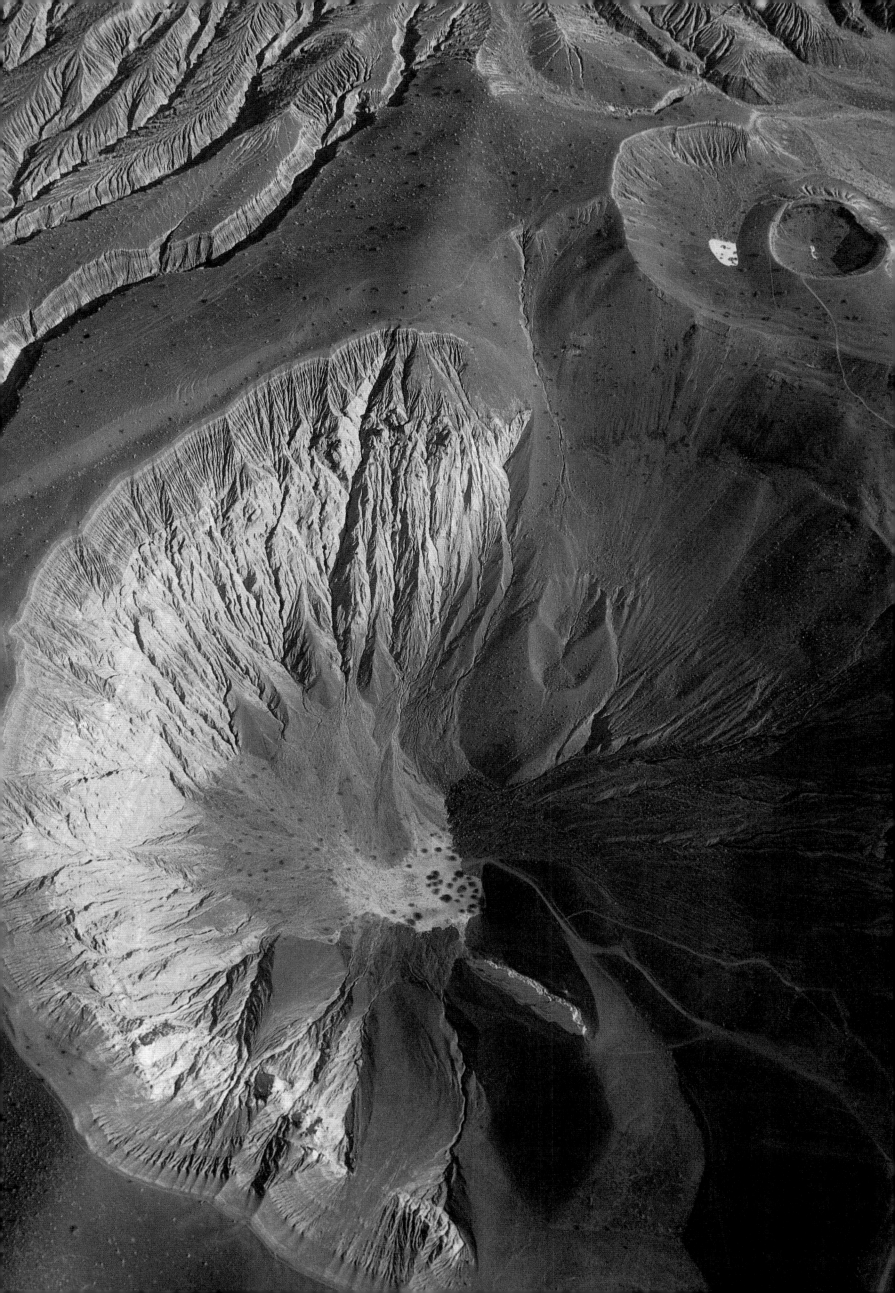

*A*bove: A stately procession of
Washingtonia filifera, the only palm
native to California, runs up a canyon
on the ancient lands of the Agua
Caliente band of the Cahuilla Indians
north of Palm Springs. *Right:* At Blythe,
near the Arizona border, a fish hatchery
flourishes in the desert heat.

The Joshua Tree (*Yucca brevifolia*) is not a tree at all, but a member of the lily family that frequently attains heights of 30 to 40 feet. The white blossoms of this giant desert flower are exquisite. Mormon pioneers are thought to have named the Joshua Tree because it reminded them of the biblical Joshua raising his arms in prayer.

Three hikers relax atop the Hidden Valley rock formations at the Joshua Tree National Monument. In days past (so legend has it) cattle rustlers hid their purloined stock among the boulders and strange rock formations of Hidden Valley. Today, visitors flock from L.A. and San Diego to enjoy the midwinter sun in this 870-square-mile reserve devoted to the protection of the desert environment.

*U*nlikely as it seems, this sand dollar-
like formation is part of a sewage
treatment plant near China Lake. Like
much of the California desert, nearby
China Lake Weapons Center is used for
military purposes.

A chemical extraction plant near
Trona extracts minerals from brine
pumped into these surface pools from
beneath the desert floor. The red color
of the mineral-rich liquid results from
the same algae that causes red tide and
the red snows in Siberia.

The Atchison, Topeka & Santa Fe arrived at Barstow in 1884 and has used it since as an important staging point for overland movement via the southern route. The Union Pacific also uses Barstow as a boxcar collection and rail-switching point.

Operated by Southern California Edison and the Los Angeles Department of Water and Power, the Solar One installation east of Daggett uses computers to rotate 1,800 mirrors (each of them 23 square feet) toward the sun. The solar heat creates steam that drives a turbine generator. Solar One serves as a reminder of the possibilities of solar energy.

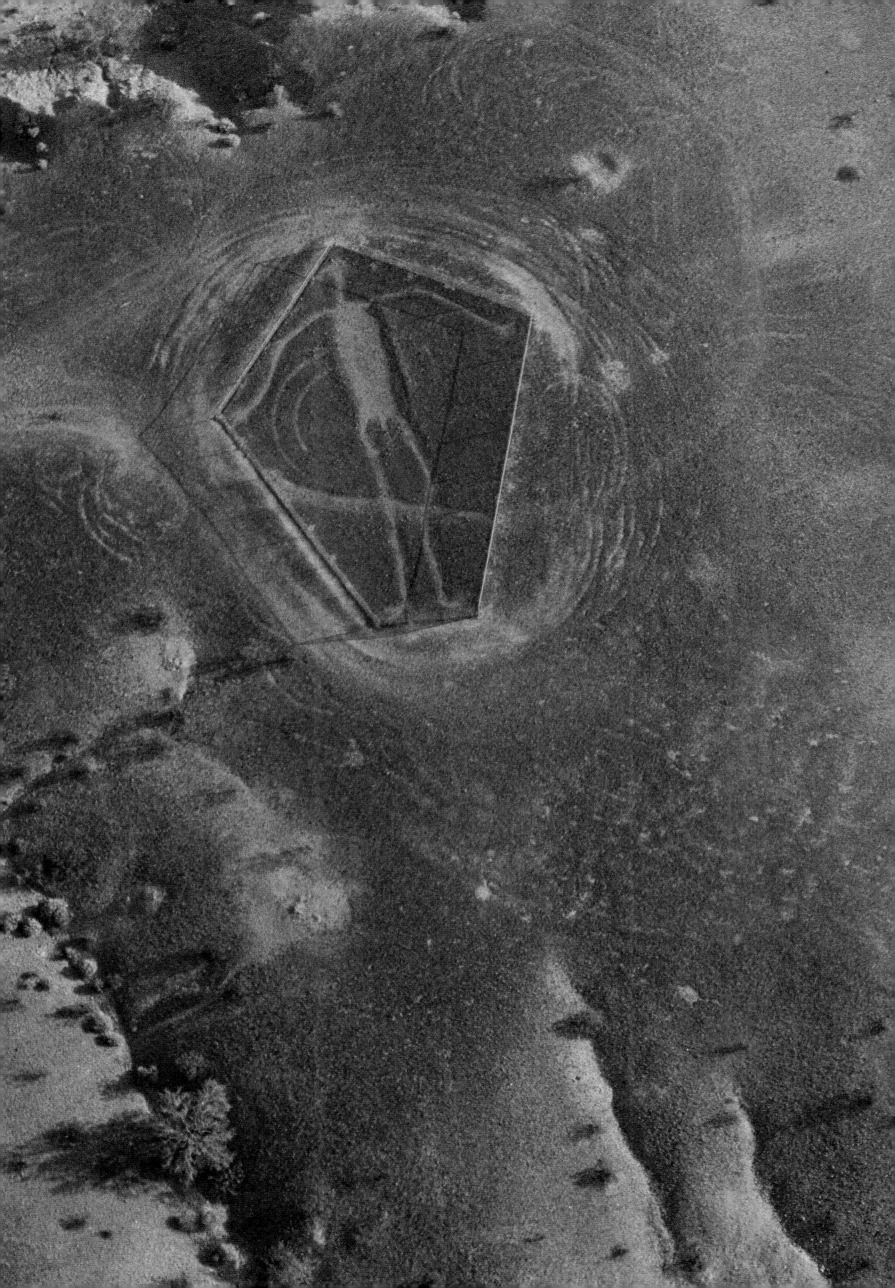

Top: Lake Havasu on the Colorado River is a 45-mile-long mecca for boaters, water skiers, and campers at the shoreline state park. *Above and left:* Intaglio pictographs lie on a rocky outcropping along the Colorado River near Blythe. They were created 500 years ago by the Pima-Papago peoples.

The space shuttle lands on a dry lake bed turned runway at Edwards Air Force Base in Kern County. Ever since World War II, the ample runways and remote location of Edwards have made it a favored test site for experimental aircraft, beginning with America's pioneer jet aircraft, the P-59, first tested here in 1942.

Truckers on I-10 near Desert Center have only the Chuckwalla Mountains in the distance to alter the monotonous landscape. During construction of the Colorado River Aqueduct in the 1930s, Desert Center became a boomtown but has since returned to its status as a genuine place in the middle of nowhere.

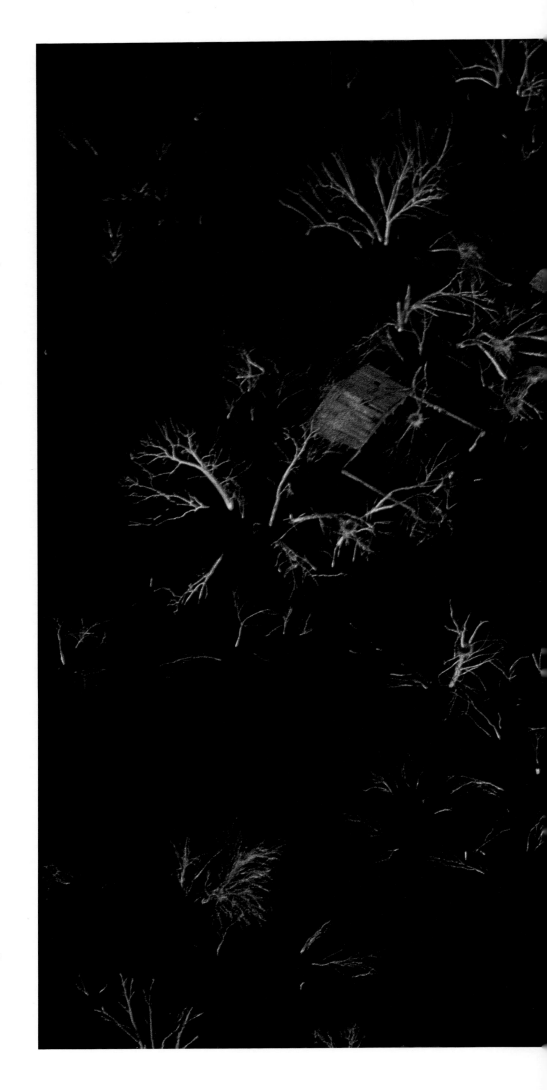

*R*anch house roofs and barren treetops reach above the surface of the Salton Sea, formed between 1905 and 1907 when an irrigation dam broke and flooded a dry lake bed north of the Imperial Valley.

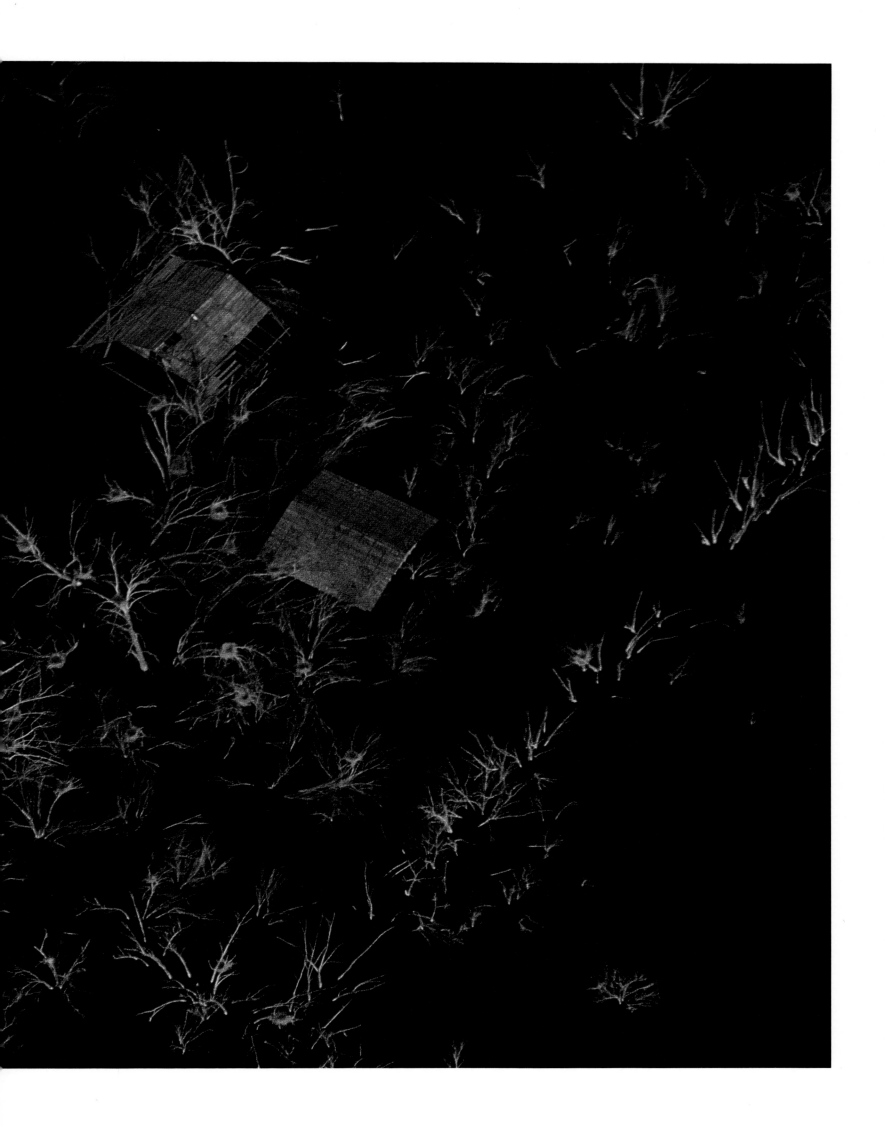

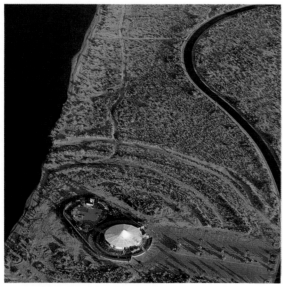

*A*bove: The Salton Sea is 30 miles long and up to 14 miles in width. Fishing and boating are currently popular along its shores. *Right:* Second-home and retirement markets have boomed the Coachella Valley, from Palm Springs to Indio, into a continuous suburban region with a population nearing the million mark.

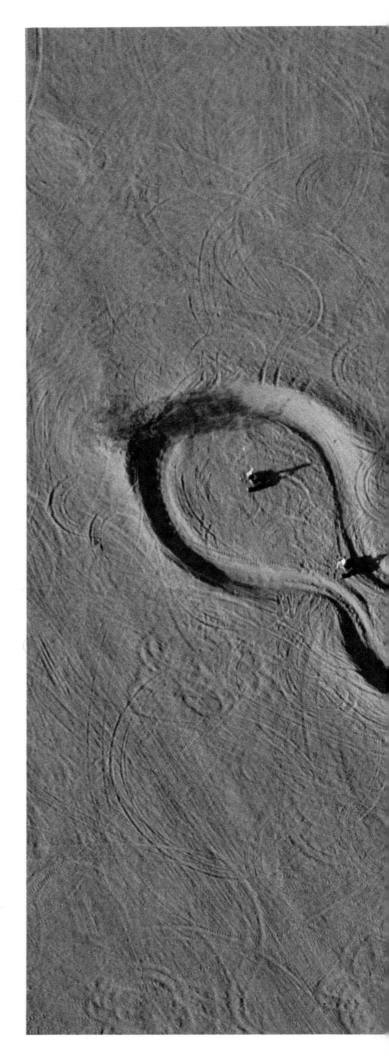

*N*othing is more luxuriant in the desert—or more capable of creating a sense of place—than water. Near Barstow on the Mojave Desert, a developer has sited homes around two man-made ponds, and the result both eludes and reaffirms the limitations of the desert environment.

*R*Vs form a circle on sand dunes near Yuma. Strained by agriculture and heavy settlement, the water resources of this portion of the desert are as unstable as the shifting sand dunes themselves.

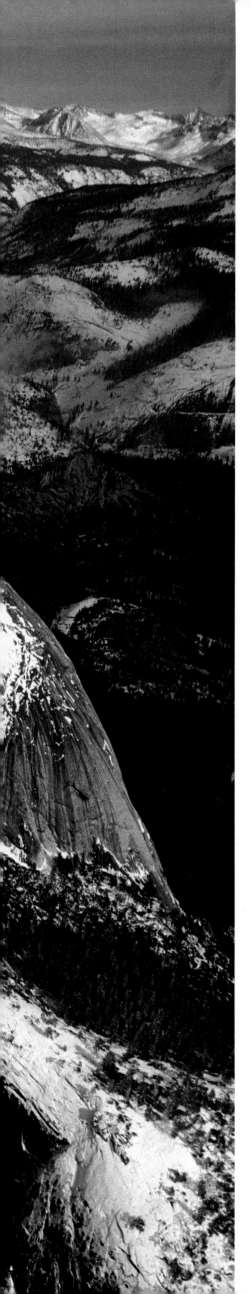

THE SIERRA NEVADA

In ages past the Miwok lived in the valley now known as Yosemite. They called their home Ahwahnee, which means "deep grassy valley." For centuries the Miwok, also known as the Awani, enjoyed the secure abundance of their seven-mile-long valley, lined by 3,000-foot granite slabs carved over the eons by stream erosion and glacial action.

Some of Joseph Walker's mountain men most likely intruded into this protected paradise in 1833, but official credit for the first discovery of the Yosemite Valley, after that of the Miwok, must be given to Major James D. Savage and Dr. L.H. Bunnell. Sadly, Savage and Bunnell were riding at the head of a hastily established Mariposa Battalion in pursuit of hostile Miwoks. On March 25, 1851, the battalion emerged from its forest trail and found

Left: Sculpted by geological and glacial action, Half Dome stands watch over Yosemite. *Above:* Like cathedral spires, these granite crags soar over Kings Canyon National Park.

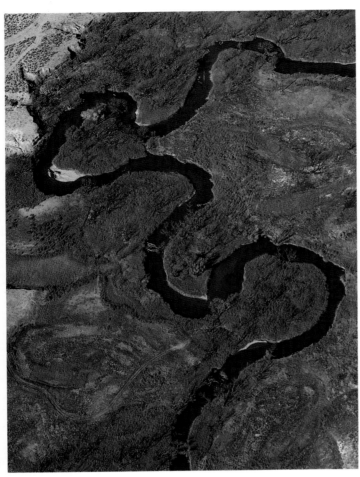

itself at a promontory which is today called Inspiration Point, overlooking the entire valley floor. "As I looked at the grandeur of the scene," Dr. Bunnell later remembered, "a peculiar exalted sensation seemed to fill my whole being and I found my eyes in tears with emotion." Bunnell named the valley Yosemite after the Miwok word for grizzly bear, *uzumati*, the valley totem.

By the 1860s, Californians were beginning to take Yosemite as their primary symbol. In June 1864 a group of Californians persuaded President Abraham Lincoln to set the Yosemite Valley and the Mariposa Big Trees aside as a preserved tract. In 1868 there arrived at Yosemite a budding naturalist by the name of John Muir, who would over the course of a half-century of ramblings, ascents, literary musings, and protectionist polemics make the Yosemite stand for everything that California promised in the way of personal growth and transformation.

In May 1903 Muir and President Theodore Roosevelt camped together for four days in Yosemite. It was one of the greatest times in Roosevelt's life, and he left a convinced conservationist. In 1906 Yosemite was ceded by California to the federal government.

Each year some two million visitors enter Yosemite. By the mid-1970s the human impact on the valley had become so pronounced that the National Park Service enacted rigid restrictions on valley usage. Still, despite these restraints, Yosemite remains a popular tourist destination. Visitors come to gaze upon Half Dome, El Capitan, Three Brothers, and Cathedral Spires, or to watch the light irradiate the sparkling spray of Ribbon, Bridal Veil, Nevada, and Vernal falls.

South of Yosemite, on the crest of the Sierra Nevada, there lived in times past another people, the Yokut, whose territory extended westward to the Fresno River and south to the Tehachapi Mountains. Because the glaciers had not scraped across this portion of the High Sierra, the sequoia trees here were very old and grew to gigantic heights. When the white man settled this region in the 1860s, he brought along smallpox, measles, and scarlet fever. By 1865 the Yokut people no longer lived beneath the arboreal giants.

Congress set aside the entire region as the Sequoia National Park in September 1890, putting it under the jurisdiction of the Army. In 1914 the Sequoia and General Grant National Parks, later renamed the Sequoia and Kings Canyon National Parks, were turned over to a precursor to the National Park Service. Averaging between 1,500 to 3,000 years in age, the Sequoia Big Trees soar more than 250 feet above the forest floor—members of an arboreal race of giants that survived the last great

Ice Age. One of the largest is the General Grant Sequoia, which is 3,000 years old and rises 267 feet above a base that is 40.3 feet in diameter. The General Sherman, in the Giant Forest in Sequoia National Park, is the largest sequoia in existence, standing 275 feet high.

After John Muir died in 1914, the state of California created the John Muir Trail from Yosemite to the headwaters of the Kern River in his honor. Terminating at Mount Whitney, the John Muir Trail moves from ridge to ridge past 148 separate peaks. Another pathway, the High Sierra Trail, constructed by the National Park Service, joins the Giant Forest with Mount Whitney. From the spring to the late fall, these trails abound with trekkers and rock climbers on expedition.

There flourishes in California a nature-oriented intellectualism, dramatically represented by John

Writer Mary Austin, who lived in the Owens Valley in the 1890s, described it as "the land of little rain."

Muir, strong enough to be considered a tradition. This sensibility prizes the mountain encounter as a moment of intense revelation, a form of philosophical probing of the relationship between human beings and the environment. One meets this sensibility in the 19th-century prose of Muir, William Brewer, Clarence King, and others, and in the photography of Eadweard Muybridge and Carleton Watkins, a tradition carried on in the 20th century by Ansel Adams and Galen Rowell. From the perspective of this tradition, the Sierra Nevada is not so much the Garden Wall as it is ground zero of a consciousness of man and nature that finds its most intense situation and imagery in the "Range of Light."

Previous pages

The Garden Wall has its most formidable component in the Sierra Nevada, also known as the Range of Light. The subtle colors of twilight over Twin Lakes on the eastern slope capture one moment in an ever-changing panorama of mountain light.

Above: Once a grassland, the Owens Valley dried up in the 20th century when waters from the Owens River were diverted south to Los Angeles. *Right:* At 7,000 years of age, Mono Lake is among the oldest lakes on the planet. L.A.'s use of streams that feed the lake has brought the water to critically low levels.

In early autumn empty ski trails spill down the snowless slopes at a Mammoth Mountain resort. Favored by Los Angelenos as the ski place of choice, the Mammoth area attracts more than 20,000 skiers to its slopes on winter weekends.

Previous pages
Mammoth Lakes glitters in the Sierran twilight west of Lee Vining. A rich vein of gold lured miners here in the 1870s.

Near Big Pine in the Owens Valley, the Palisades portion of the White Mountains stand guard on the high ground of the Garden Wall.

Whitney Portal Road leads to the base of Mount Whitney, the highest peak in the contiguous United States.

"How glorious a greeting the sun gives the mountains! . . . The highest peaks burned like islands in a sea of liquid shade. Then the lower peaks and spires caught the glow, and long leaves of light, streaming through many a notch and pass, fell thick on the frozen meadows."

— John Muir,
The Mountains of California

THE PROJECT

*P*roject director Robert Cave-Rogers (shirtless) confers with pilot Mike Cummings as they make final engine adjustments before venturing over the High Sierra.

Like aerial archaeologists, pilot Mike Cummings and photographer Reg Morrison surveyed more than 23,000 miles to uncover the images that appear in *Over California*. Their flight path crossed every county and city in the state, in an airborne odyssey that sought to bring back for the eyes of earthbound mortals the extraordinary insights and visions normally reserved for those who fly.

Flying in a specially modified de Havilland Beaver equipped with wide-angle bubble windows and amphibious floats, photographer and pilot took to the air, guided by a shoot list specially prepared by author Kevin Starr and research editor Barbara Roether to exemplify the social and geographic diversity of California.

"Geographic diversity" is photographer Reg Morrison's stock in trade. A week prior to his arrival among the glass-walled canyons of Los Angeles, Reg was "living in a bogged car in the middle of the flooded Simpson desert in Australia. One minute I was coping with total isolation and immobility, the next I was in a helicopter maneuvering between the skyscrapers of one of the world's largest cities.

"In California, I found all the visual scales had changed, as had the angles of the sun I was accustomed to—in South Australia, a winter sun at midday is in the northern sky. The photographic imperatives were also new—the tight geometry of intensive agriculture, the embryonic urban sprawl. And saddening to the environmentalist in me, as well as the photographer, was the man-made haze that hung in the sky to mar so many otherwise beautiful landscapes. But overlooking it all was the Sierra Nevada, and since Australia is the billiard table of continents, I often felt like a kid in a candy store."

The *Over California* photo team worked a strenuous daily regime. Pilot Mike Cummings would open a sleepy eye at 4:30 A.M. to check the dawn cloud level and call the airports to establish visibili-ty along the day's proposed flight path. He and Reg made two flights a day, one at dawn and the second in the late afternoon, when shadows were long and deep. Reg sat on the aircraft floor behind the pilot, surrounded by three (always loaded) 35mm Nikons and two Pentax 5x4 cameras. Peering from side to side like a hungry eagle scanning for prey, he would give directions via headset to Mike at the controls, so that in effect pilot and aircraft became a flying tripod for Reg's cameras.

For pilot Mike Cummings, whose experience includes nearly ten years piloting in the notoriously hazardous Alaskan wilderness, *Over California* was "easily the most unusual flying assignment I'd ever had. It quickly became evident that straight-line 'point A to

BARBARA ROETHER

*T*he unexpected usefulness of amphibious floats in the Mojave Desert is demonstrated here as pilot Mike Cummings (*left*) and photographer Reg Morrison consult their charts.

point B' flying was not on the agenda. Instead, my course was continually interrupted by Reg's pleas to 'Circle left-hand,' 'Fly up sun,' 'Lift your left wing,' and, repeatedly, 'Can we fly a little lower?'"

Apart from the usual difficulties associated with flying an aircraft, including finding landing strips and aviation fuel in some of the state's more remote corners, Mike dealt with a host of other

L.A. pilot Chuck Street (*above*) and Hayward pilot Jim Larsen ferried Reg via helicopter over larger cities for close-up camera work.

challenges. Federal aviation altitude restrictions did not always coincide with the photographer's creative needs, nor did air-traffic jams near metropolitan airports like LAX. Extra risks came with maneuvering through several military bombing and gunnery practice ranges, and attempting close-ups in narrow Sierra canyons, or being forced down several hundred stomach-churning feet in an air pocket over Death Valley.

Altogether the team spent more than 200 hours in the air, including five hours of helicopter shooting in Los Angeles and San Francisco. The first part of the expedition, in November and December 1988, covered the northern and central regions of the state. A springtime shoot, in April and May 1989, covered the southern deserts and the coastline.

Every take-off, every flight, was accompanied with the promise of discovering something unexpected, something serendipitous along the flight

path—a giraffe in a green meadow in San Diego, an ocean-going freighter amid the fruit trees of the Central Valley. There was a special thrill in searching for the ancient intaglio pictographs the photo team knew were hidden somewhere along the mountain slopes of the Colorado River. Suddenly they appeared, horses and men as clear as the day they were drawn, like messages left in expectation of eventual discovery: civilizations talking across a millennium, one technology to the other.

Often the crew marveled at the seamless horizon—the view that extended beyond a single context, beyond a street and a neighborhood and a town, connecting one city to the next; the way in which towns seem to grow out of the land, the way rivers seek their outlets in the sea.

Thus after a year of work, the aerial archaeologists of *Over California* offer their discoveries to the people of California: Eureka, we have found it!

Aviator Steve Pfister flies over Santa Monica in a 1938 Howard DGA-11.

ACKNOWLEDGMENTS

The producers of *Over California* would like to thank the following individuals and institutions for their assistance:

Beverley Barnes; Richard Allison; David and Camille Bruce; Frank Etter at Ads Aloft, South Lake Tahoe; Jim Larsen of Jim Larsen Helicopters at Hayward; Pamela MacInnes-Stine; Professor Daniel McCarthy, Department of Archeology, University of California at Irvine; Frank Norris; Steve Pfister; Peter Pierson; Howard "Hap" Plumm of American Aerial Surveys, Inc. at Sacramento Executive Airport; Jack Stewart at the California Department of Commerce; Chuck Street; Francis "Chub" Trainor and his red Howard DGA-11; Susan and Vilmos Zsigmond; the air traffic controllers at Edwards Air Force Base; Neptune's Palace and Tarantinos, Fisherman's Wharf, San Francisco; New Lab of San Francisco; The Camera Exchange of Van Nuys; The Tournament of Roses Association, Pasadena; and the kind aviators at the small airports throughout California, especially in Barstow, Crescent City, Columbia, Oceanside, Ramona, Salinas, Santa Paula, and Van Nuys.

INDEX